A SYLLABUS FOR BLACK WOMEN:

110 LIFE LESSONS FOR SISTAHS IN COLLEGE

Thaïs D. Bass-Moore

DEDICATION

For my daughters and all the women in FLI.

CONTENTS

ACKNOWLEDGMENTS

Wow! I finally did it. I wrote this book eight years before ever picking it back up again. So, I'll start with acknowledging myself for pulling it from the shelf, dusting it off, and finishing it! But of course, I could not have done it without people encouraging me. If I fail to thank everyone who deserves recognition, please forgive me. Thank you, Chelsea Jones, for reading the manuscript in its rawest form years ago and providing feedback. Thank you, LaShawn Washington, for telling me to pull it off the shelf. Thank you, Leonard Moore, for giving me amazing ideas. Thank you, Margot Starbuck, for editing the book's content—what great insight you have. Raven Pierre, thank you for the final touches and ideas that made it feel complete. José Granados, thank you for helping me to get the cover uploaded! Thank you to the women of the Fearless Leadership Institute at the University of Texas at Austin, who provide me with a platform to live this stuff out in front of. You keep me accountable. To all my friends, I live to laugh and grow with you all. To all my siblings and cousins who poured into me my whole life—every time I think of you I cry because I love you all so much and it's hard living so far from you for so long. Mom, I love you. Because of your prayers, I am who I am today. Dad, I miss you terribly, but I'm so glad you're in heaven, fishing, hunting and enjoying the goodness of the Lord. Again, thank you Leonard, my boo, my lover, my blessing, my best friend, my confidant, my advisor—you've made me better. Thank you Jaaucklyn, Lauryn, and Len—for loving me and being my best friends. All three of you give me so much life and laughter. What would I do without you? Go be who God created you to be! And remember that God loves you more than I do. And finally, to God the Father, Jesus his Son, and the Holy Spirit—you wooed me, snatched me up and changed my life. Thank you for choosing me and using me!

Thank you to the anonymous artist for the amazing illustration I used for the cover.

PREFACE

You may not agree with everything written in this book. That's okay. It may not be for you. This is just my perspective. I didn't write it for anyone's approval. I simply wrote about my life experiences, what I learned from them, and what I believe to be good choices. My passion is for women to live more productive and fruitful lives than I did in when I was in college. Some of the stories shared in this book are my own and some are from other women I know and love.

INTRODUCTION

Do you realize that words have power? Whether in our thoughts or out loud, the words we think and say about ourselves and others can become our reality. Words have the power to build up and tear down. Words have the power to bring together and to separate. Words have the power to create and to destroy. For example, if I were your mother or your good friend, and I told you that you are beautiful and that I love you—that would make you smile, and you would probably feel warm feelings about yourself and me. On the flip, if I said to you that I hate you and I wish that you never existed that would probably hurt you to your core. The same is true for the words we speak about our own selves. If I say to myself constantly, things like—*I'm ugly* or *I hate myself* or *nobody loves me*—eventually I'll believe it and my life will more than likely resemble my words. But if I say things like—*I am beautiful, I am blessed, I am successful, I am loved*—over time my life will begin to reflect those words more and more. We tend to act in accordance with our words and our life becomes shaped by them.

It took me years to grasp these concepts.

I never thought I was enough. As a child, I got hurt,

and then hurt again as a teenager. As I grew into my adulthood, I was very insecure and didn't think very highly of myself. My insecurity showed itself in the choices I made, how I treated others and how I treated myself. I was told over and over again in various ways that I was too skinny and that I didn't have enough butt and that I looked like a pelican and more. All of these humiliations stuck with me and over time I believed them. I accepted them as truth when really, they were lies. I began to make bad decisions in relationships, decisions that showed my lack of self-worth. *Wow*, I thought, *someone is attracted to me—maybe I am sexy, maybe I am enough*. But when the relationship turned bad which it did time and time again, I ended up feeling worse about myself. I was trying to find my value and self-worth in relationships not realizing it could never be found there. In fact, my insecurities worsened instead of getting better. It got so bad, that I hated myself. My life sucked and I no longer wanted to live.

God intervened. It took a lot of years and tears, as well as encouragement and prayers from others, for me to begin to see myself as worthy of love and life. When I think about what ultimately transformed my life, it was after a near death experience where I almost drowned in the Pacific Ocean. During the time of the incident I was suicidal but when I almost drowned, while body surfing, and was miraculously rescued, God spoke into my life. He told me, *Thaïs, I love you. It is not your time to go. I created you on purpose for a purpose. I'll decide when it is your time to go. Until then, I have some amazing things for you to accomplish.* It was more of an impression than an actual voice that I heard. That same day that I was rescued from drowning, I gave my life to Christ. My life didn't change right away. In fact, that was twenty years ago, and I'm still in the process of changing for the better. It's a journey—one that I'm glad I decided to take.

My hope is that every woman would see herself as the beautiful and powerful woman that she was created to be. I wish that every woman would learn the power of her words and thoughts about herself and others. I wish that she could recognize that she holds the power to build up or tear down. She has the power to bring together and the power to separate. You, that is, have the power to create and the power to destroy. And it all starts with your thoughts.

You see, our thoughts become our words and our words become our beliefs and our beliefs become our actions and our actions become our lifestyle and our lifestyle becomes who we are. What are your thoughts? What are your words? Are they providing you with life or destruction?

If you are someone who...

- wants advice on how to navigate college
- wants to make better choices
- struggles with insecurity
- wants to learn to love yourself
- seems to find yourself involved in repetitive toxic relationships
- confused about your identity
- pretends to be someone else just to fit in
- wakes up every day and dreads getting out of bed
- is scared of what tomorrow holds
- desires a closer relationship with God

...then this book is for you.

It gets real, but don't let that scare you. I hope the following 110 lessons containing my words of wisdom will encourage you to make better choices. Because that's really all it's about...making better choices. I'd love to save you from making some of the mistakes that I, or my friends, made. Those bad choices led to a bad life in which I no longer wanted to exist. Now, on this, my current journey, I have learned to love life and love myself. I am gradually learning to love exactly how God created me and increasingly looking forward to each day. If you have similar hang-ups in life that keep you from completely liking yourself or enjoying life, I hope and pray that will change for you like it has for me. I think this book could be of assistance to you. Please enjoy. #1 is my favorite!

PART 1
PERSONAL STUFF

#1 Unconditional Love

God loves you so much. There is nothing you can do that would make him love you any more than he already does. There is nothing you can do that would make him love you any less. He can't help but love you, because *God is love*. He created you on purpose. He created you when he did, no sooner or later, because now is the time that he needs you. He wasn't having a bad day when he created you. Everything about you was intentional. So, go ahead and accept yourself. Love yourself. And remember, you are loved.

#2 Who Am I?

Take time to get to know yourself. Spend time alone writing out your likes and dislikes. Are you one of those students who walks around campus with earbuds in your ear throughout the day? Do you go from class to class with your eyes on your phone? Do you always need noise or someone around? I encourage to take quiet time and get to know yourself. Sometimes it can be uncomfortable to be alone with ourselves, with only our thoughts, but those are opportunities to grow and get to know yourself better. Use that time to write out your dreams and desires. Write out what hurts you and what brings you joy. Journal. Write about your good days and your bad ones. What made them good? What made them bad? Write about it. Recognize both the good and the bad but remember to set your focus on the good. When you focus on good things, it creates joy. When you focus on negative things, it tends to make you more negative. So why write about the negative, right? Because you want to get it out. Don't hold it in. You want to make sense of it. You can learn from it. What made it bad? What can you do differently the next time? What about yourself, your actions or inactions need to change so that it won't happen again or so that it won't bother you again?

Write about your strengths and your weaknesses. Then go back later, maybe six months or so, and read it. See if there was any growth. In this way your journal serves as a before and after picture. Do this and hopefully you will see progress. If there was no progress then write down what you can do to generate progress, to create change. You have the power to shape your life. Over time, you will begin to understand yourself better. What makes you tick, what makes you tock! Get to know you—the REAL you.

One of the ways I get to know myself better is by getting to *know* my Creator better. I believe God created me, so it just makes sense that he should know a thing or two about me. I spend time with God by talking to him, by listening to him, by taking a nature walk and enjoying his creativity, by singing songs to him and about him, and of course by reading my Bible and other books that serve as a tool to help me understand the Bible better. Notice I didn't mention attending church as a way to become closer to God. Yes, I believe church is a great place to learn more about God and to fellowship with others, however getting to know God on a personal level takes one-on-one time.

It is essential to know who you are, so that you know where you are going in life and why you're going there.

#3 Wounded, Hurt & Depressed
Who hurt you?

You ever feel like your life is cursed? Or you've been framed? Or like things just don't work well for you—EVER? Well, you don't just wake up one morning and choose to have a tragic life. You didn't roll out of bed and simply choose depression. You didn't have dreams as a little girl that you would grow up to be miserable. No, that's not usually how it works. There is usually a cause. More than likely someone hurt you. Someone hurt you so bad—it injured you to your core. And, unfortunately if you didn't take any action to obtain healing from this great hurt, then you inadvertently chose to live with the pain. It was too hard to climb up and out of the pain. Too hard to pull away from the circumstances, so you decided to remain *there* and make the most of it—you thought that would be easier. Was this the place you imagined being when you were a little girl playing with your dolls or bouncing the ball? Is this the life you imagined when you fantasized about your future? If you are at a low point in your life right now, then more than likely there was a cause. You may think that it's easier to remain in your current circumstance and just deal with it, rather than climb your way out of this low place and figure out a better way. Is that what you think—that it's easier to remain?

No baby, this is not you. YOU are inside of there—somewhere. Wounded. Hiding. Too scared to come out. Your dreams for a wonderful life are still in there somewhere. Someone hurt you, but you were never meant to remain in that hurt. Someone hurt you, but you can come out of that drama, that pain, that box, that situation.

#4 Allow God to Heal Your Broken Heart

The image above reminds me of my heart and how God has healed me. Look at the heart shaped rock in the center of the photo. Notice on the right, that the top part of the heart has been broken, but there are no jagged edges. It's all been smoothed out. I feel like that's what God did to my heart—the areas that were broken, he smoothed them out. The way its left, broken but smooth, serves as a reminder for where I was and what God did for me. That area of my life has been smoothed out by God's love, grace and forgiveness. And then notice the part of the heart that has a hole in it. People, circumstances, and bad choices dug a hole in my life. But God came and filled in that hole and covered the void with this love. The heart doesn't look perfect, but it does look resilient and taken care of. If God had made the heart look perfect and untouched, I might forget what He did for me; I might forget to share my story of redemption, restoration, and salvation. Instead I'm reminded that God is good and that he loves me. And that's something I want to exclaim to the world!

#5 Are You Easily Angered?

Are you easily angered? Do the smallest situations set you off? Maybe you have a smart-ass answer for everything and you're ready to go off on someone, anyone, the moment they cross you. No one gets a pass. Is this true for you? If so, you have to learn how to control your anger. Figure out why you are so mad. Who pissed you off? Who hurt you? Anger is often a sign of rejection. Did someone reject you and now you harbor hurt and anger in your life? CHOOSE to forgive that person and move on with your life. Anger will hold you down and cause you to walk in a circle where there is no progress being made. Anger can lead to d*anger*. It can be an enemy. Anger rarely brings about good results. Of course, you should get angry over injustices and poverty and mass incarceration and other dehumanizing circumstances! But choose to act on those issues in ways that will be productive. The anger I'm referring to here is more about having anger in your heart or having an angry personality or being known for flippin' off. That type of anger is unhealthy. It may feel good for the moment, but everything that feels good isn't always good.

Learn to control your anger. Remind yourself that no one is perfect, and everyone is capable of hurting you or offending you whether intentionally or not. Give people the benefit of the doubt. Maybe they didn't mean it like that or maybe they did, but you can't allow what people do or don't do to control how you respond. You must control your response. You cannot react to everything. You need to let some things slide. The more you do this, the more peace and emotional stability you will have—the more you can enjoy your life. If it's not something that you can just let slide—if it's bigger than that, then deal with it. Talk to the person about how they hurt you. Read books on how to forgive and deal with your anger. Don't just walk around angry. You can change that. Choose better.

#6 Journal Entry

I remember this one night at the club. She pissed me off! I was at the bar and this guy was trying to get my number. I didn't really want to give him my number, but he was nice, and I didn't want to hurt his feelings, so I decided to give him a fake number. (Oops, not nice.) I asked the bartender for a pen, to write down my number with, and when she handed it to me, she called me a b**ch. I'm not sure why she did that, but it pissed me off. So, I waited until after I wrote down my number and handed the pen back to her and said, "Thank you b**ch." She said something back, I could barely hear because the music was so loud, but I'm sure it wasn't anything nice, so I reached over the bar and picked up the beer fountain spray thingy and sprayed it at her. The next thing I know, the security guard was headed my direction. My friends saw what was going on and intercepted me before the guards got to me and shoved me out of the club. I was cussin' and fussin', talking about how I was gone f**k her up and how she better be glad my friends pushed me out. We got out the club and ran to the car and drove off before the security could reach us. We laughed about it later. But thinking back, I did stuff like that all the time. Couldn't nobody say nothing to me without me saying something back, or swinging on them, or doing something crazy. Glad I never got caught. Looking back, I had serious anger issues. I realize now that being angry was a sort of comfort zone for me. It's what I was used to. Thank you, God for helping me to let go of that anger and get to the root of what was hurting me.

#7 Life is a Series of Choices

When I was growing up, I was not taught about the **power of choice**. My parents either told me *No!* or they gave me that look that said *if you don't stop, I will hurt you*. Or if they deemed necessary, they would spank me. But never did they sit with me and teach me that life is all about choices. They didn't explain to me that a series of good choices will ultimately lead to a good life and a series of bad choices will lead to a bad life. Looking back, my high school and young adult life was bad. It got so bad that I hated life. But I didn't realize that it was caused from making a series of bad choices. I would constantly cuss people out, and if I felt threatened or attacked, I would always seek revenge. I would lie, cheat, steal, and bully, and then wonder why I was always looking over my shoulder. I was always getting in trouble and was always involved in challenging relationships. I had to learn the hard way.

Now that I know, I try to make good choices in everything I do, everything I say, and everything I think. As a result, I can wholeheartedly say my life is good. I choose to let people off the hook (most of the time), speak kind words to people, encourage others, and tell the truth. I intentionally think about what I can do to make others smile. In turn, I have joy and experience healthier relationships. I have a good life and I enjoy it. Of course, I make mistakes and don't always get it right, but I am aware that in EVERY situation I have options available to me. I used to just let life happen to me and I'd act and react however I felt in the moment. I now realize that I can choose my words and actions wisely.

Take control over your life, your thoughts, your actions and reactions. You have the power to make good choices that will better you and will positively impact those around you.

#8 Don't Trust Your Feelings
Your feelings cannot be trusted. Joyce Meyer, an

amazing evangelist, once said, *feelings are fickle*. Because feelings are fickle, we cannot live life based upon the way we feel. We must honor God and do what is right no matter what our feelings may say. How many times have you felt like slapping someone in the face? How often have you wanted to cuss your mother out? How often have you wanted to miss class because you just didn't feel like it? How often have you wanted to go off on your roommate because they left soiled dishes in the sink? How often have you wanted to send your professor an email telling her how boring her lectures are? We can't do everything we feel. You may have a valid reason to do all the things mentioned above, but will those things lead to a good outcome or an ugly or even dangerous outcome?

So often in life, we don't take the time to think before we speak or before we act or react to something. We just do what comes naturally. I lived that way for most of my life and wondered why I was always in bad situations. I thought it was because other people did me wrong and it was *their* fault that I had to cuss them out, or it was *their* fault I had to take one to the jaw, or it was *their* fault I ignored them for a week.

Although a person may have wronged you, you can pause and choose the best reaction. Notice I said pause, then choose. Choosing to do what is right in a situation usually takes a moment to stop yourself and think: *What is the best thing for me to do here?* OR *What kind of outcome do I want?* OR *What is at stake here?* When you PAUSE and ask yourself one of these questions and respond honestly and earnestly, more often than not, you will make a good choice. And at first, at least in my case, pausing and making the better choice will not be easy, but with time and lots of practice, it will become easier. You shouldn't allow what you *feel* like doing to control you. As for me, I don't want my feelings to be my god. I don't want to be enslaved to them. Instead, I want to honor God and do what makes Him smile.

#9 Eat Better

Start making healthy food choices. Instead of buying a bag of chips and a pickle, grab an apple, banana, or a peach. Or even some peanuts. Instead of buying a Fanta or a Coke, get some water or a fruit 'n veggie smoothie. If you live in an area where healthy food is not readily available, you may have to spend a bit more time and go to an area that sells healthy food options. Making healthy food choices will give you energy, grant you healthier skin and hair, keep your bowels regular, help you to have a nice physique, and ultimately prolong your youthfulness and vitality.

Most importantly, drink lots of water. Say no to sweetened water or as the old folks used to say, *sugar water*, and other artificially flavored drinks and get drunk on H2O. Your body will love you for it!

#10 The Liberating Power of Exercise

Get active. Walk. Jog. Run. Exercise. Do Zumba. Do Yoga. Dance. Lift Weights. Stretch. Move. Don't sit all day long. You will become old and out of shape sooner than you'd like. You may not be the exercising type, but you don't have to be. Just do it. It's challenging getting started, but once you get up and do even just 10 minutes of some sort of movement, your body will appreciate you. You may be sore afterwards but that's because you rarely or possibly never use those muscles. Use them. Get in shape. You'll feel better physically, mentally, emotionally, and spiritually. You see, our body is all connected. When you improve physically it can't help but improve you mentally, emotionally and spiritually. The same is true for if you focus on enriching your spiritual life—it will impact every other area of your life. Getting in shape also helps you to be more confident and secure in who you are, because you are taking care of your body. You may think that you don't have enough time in your day to exercise or you can't afford a gym membership. Ten minutes on your living room floor is very doable. You can even click on an online work-out link to follow along with, or just have a regimen where you do so many jumping jacks, sit-ups, push-ups, and lunges each day and then every week increase the amount by 5 or 10. Before it gets dark, go take a 10-minute walk or jog or "wog", as my friends and I call it. Ask a friend to go with you if that helps you feel safer.

Also, you can have an accountability partner to check-in with you to make sure you did your 10 minutes each day. Next week make it 15 minutes. And if you happen to skip a day because you got busy or it slipped your mind, that's okay, do it the next day. Make it a new habit in your life. You'll love yourself for it!

#11 Go to Bed

Go to bed. Unless you are working on a major project, or assignment, then stop staying up so late. Your body needs rest. Give yourself a specific bedtime and stick to it. If you cut out a bulk of the time you spend on social media, you'll have more hours in the day to handle responsibilities, to be active, and to have adequate rest and sleep time. But you have to use discipline. It's not just going to happen on its own. You have to choose to go to bed at a decent time and then commit to doing so—and that may mean altering your habits or addictions.

#12 Growing Pains

Keep growing. Keep making better choices.

WARNING: GROWING PAINS WILL OCCUR.

Regardless of growing pains, choose the path of growth. I'm not sure about you, but I'd rather have pain as a result of growing rather than the pain that accompanies stagnation.

Be sure to read the small print below:

Growing pains can occur when you are making necessary changes in your life in order to have a better life. These changes can sometimes make for discomfort or grief. For example, say you know you need to get someone out of your life. So, you finally muster up enough courage to do so, which can be extremely hard to do. And then the fear and loneliness you may experience after that person is gone can be overwhelming. But you know it's for the best and you heard it will get better. Stick with that. It *will* get better. You're just in transition mode, but you made a good choice. You're growing. It may be painful, but it's worth it!

#13 What's Your Passion?

What are you passionate about?

Go after it.

I'm not talking about a guy.

I'm talking about something that you do, that when you do it no one can stop you. You feel dynamic. You feel radiant. You feel creative. You feel like you're making an impact.

What's that thing that brings you joy when you do it and gives joy to those who are around you? What's that thing that seems meaningful to you and others?

Whatever that is, that's your passion. Pursue it. That's what you were created to do.

If you feel as though you don't have that kind of passion for anything, then be willing to try new things until you find it. Don't live in a box. Be willing to explore, as long as it doesn't bring harm to you or to others.

What if you have more than one passion? Then do them all; not necessarily at the same time though.

You have a long life ahead of you, so spread your passions out. Choose what's best and most contributory to pursue in this season of your life. Do it and do it well. Then go for the next passion in another season of your life. And then the next. You have time. You don't have to rush. I promise you. You have time.

For example, three of the many things I'm passionate about are family, Black women, and theatre. Trying to pursue all three of those at one time, would leave me tired and empty. Although there is some overlap, I chose to give each one it's divided attention. I stayed at home for ten years and raised my children. After the ten years at home, I started working at the University of Texas at Austin; out of my love for Black women, I developed a holistic development program for them at the university. Next, I'm off to Broadway. Each passion will take time, commitment and development. But I plan to accomplish and fulfill my purpose in all three areas—never leaving anyone of them behind, but just offering more to one at a specific time.

#14 Write the Vision
What are some of your dreams and goals? Write them down on a sheet of paper and tape that paper

to your mirror or your laptop or somewhere where you will see it often. If you write them down, you are more likely to pursue them and accomplish them. I've researched the science to how much writing down ideas is a determining factor in whether the ideas actualize. Some of the benefits to writing down your thoughts are that:

- it frees up mind-space so that you can relax
- it keeps your mind sharp
- it helps you to think BIGGER

Here's the URL for further information on the benefits of writing things down:

(https://www.shopify.com/content/6-psychological-benefits-of-writing-things-down)

Think about something as simple as your grocery list. If you write down all the items that you need before going to the store, you will more than likely leave the store with all the items that you wrote on the list. However, if you choose not to write a grocery list, you will more than likely return home with only some of the things that you needed (and with some additional items that you didn't need). Writing it keeps it before you. Writing it reminds you. Writing it encourages you. You can write in your journal. Or write it and stick it to your mirror or refrigerator where you will see it every day. You can even write it and stick it in your Bible. Or on your laptop. But write it. Right now. Stop and write.

#15 Just Ask

Sometimes we don't accomplish our goals because we don't know *what to do* or *how to do it*. The internet is at your fingertips. Do a search and find out the first three steps in pursuing your dreams. Some websites may vary on the advice they give, but you can choose what works best for you. Take the first step. Then the next. No excuses. Keep going.

Let's say you want to own and operate a food truck that serves breakfast. Do a search on the internet for "how to own and operate a food truck." A lot of websites will give you a list of instructions along with some testimonials from individuals who have done this very thing. Create a to-do list in your journal and number the list from 1 to 10 (or whatever number brings you to completion) and then begin completing the said list starting with number 1. Once you have accomplished number 1, cross it off your list to indicate that it has been completed. Then proceed to number 2 on the list and do it! Again, once you have accomplished number 2, cross it off your list and move to number 3. Continue with this method until you have reached your goal. Will interruptions and mistakes happen along the way? Yes indeed. Don't let those be roadblocks, but just situations that you must learn and grown from. Keep reaching and pressing towards your goal. If your goal gets altered along the way, that's fine. Sometimes our desires get fine-tuned and stretched as we get closer to them.

In addition to tackling your to-do list, seek out other food truck owners in order to gain real-life tips and advice—advice the internet may not give you. Find out the startup costs. Find out what you need lined up to get started. Find out how to create a business plan. Gain all the knowledge you can. But don't get fat off of knowledge and sit on it. Move! Do what you need to do. The world is waiting on the food truck (or whatever it is you're wanting to do)—they hungry! Feed them what the good Lord gave you! If you don't do what you have in your heart to do (which is your calling), there will be a void in society.

I want to reiterate that no matter what your desire is, find someone who is already doing it. Ask them what they did to get there. Ask to shadow them for a day or two, or even longer, to see if it is something you really want to pursue. Wisdom is within your reach. You don't have to go about achieving your goals blindly. Ask for help. Ask for advice. Reach your goals.

#16 Failing Forward

We all make mistakes in life. It's a part of being human. It's a part of learning. It's a part of growing up. You are not a failure because of your mistakes. Instead of being discouraged, use what you have learned from that mistake to do better the next time and to help someone else not to make the same.

I had to change my major while in school at UCLA because my GPA was dropping. I probably would have been okay if I knew how to navigate college resources better and get the necessary help I needed. But I just didn't know how. I felt like a failure for having to change my major. I went to school so that I could graduate and go to medical school to become an OB/GYN, but I failed. I considered dropping out of school. But instead, I had taken a class in African American history a year or so prior and loved it. I was informed that I could change my major to African American studies with a concentration in English. I graduated magna cum laude. And look at me now, I'm using both African American studies and English—I *wrote* this book for *African American* women. I fell in love with our history as a people, because it helped me to understand where we are as a people today. I've used the knowledge of our rich history to write and direct plays and I created a sustainable program at the University of Texas at Austin for Black women to build them holistically. All because I learned our history and understood what it would take to reverse the hands of time, which are love and knowledge. Or shall I say God and education. What I considered a loss, God used for good, and pushed me into my purpose and destiny! I may not be a medical doctor, but I've helped many young Black women at UT on their path from undergrad school to medical school.

#17 The Danger of Nursing Insecurities

Go places, watch stuff, and read things that will make you feel better about yourself, instead of, going places, watching stuff, and reading things that feed your insecurities. For example, most of my life I've been insecure about my butt. I've always been told by friends, relatives and media that as a Black woman, I'm supposed to have a bigger butt. I believed that lie, therefore, I was insecure for most of my life. Over time, I've learned that I can't watch and listen to things that nourish the lie, otherwise, it grows. I must be very intentional about what I absorb and don't absorb. I have to protect myself. Therefore, there are certain songs, websites, TV shows, magazines and more that I don't subscribe to.

Instead I absorb literature and music that tells me that I am beautiful just the way God made me.

#18 What Flowers Teach Us About Life

One of my favorite quotes is: *A flower doesn't think of competing with the flower next to it. It just blooms.*

In other words, all the women in your life are like flowers—beautiful and purposeful. You don't need to try to be better than them or more beautiful than them. Every flower I've seen is beautiful and makes me smile. So just be you. That's beautiful and powerful enough.

#19 Avoid D.A.s

You are loved. God loves you and you are never alone. I know sometimes we just want someone around. Someone to be close. But we can't be so desperate to fill that void that we end up having certain individuals around us who will use us. Don't allow the need and yearning to be with someone, to lead you to do things that defile you or your relationship with God. Choose wisely who you spend time with. Choose wisely what you do. Have boundaries established for what you will and won't do and stick to it. For example, you might establish that, *I will not make a dick appointment*—aka D.A.

(Back in my day we called it a "booty call.") Or, *I will not make a P.A. either.* (I'll let you figure that one out.) That's an established boundary—you've laid down a rule for yourself for what you will not do before the opportunity even presents itself. That way, when the opportunity does present itself, you already have the answer—*No, I don't do those.* Or, you might say, I will go to the party and dance and have a good time and have no more than one drink. That's another boundary. You have given yourself permission to have fun, but without going too far.

#20 Be More, Be You

If you want more from life than what you are currently experiencing, then choose to be all of who you were created to be. Do what you were created to do. Stop shrinking. Stop settling for less. Stop making excuses. Go be!

Sometimes we choose not to shine because we don't want all eyes on us. Or sometimes we don't want others to feel like we think we are better than them, so we don't give it our all—we hold back. Or sometimes we don't feel like our input or output is sufficient or adequate, so we pull back and don't give anything. Stop second guessing yourself. Stop worrying about what others will think about what you bring to the table. If you don't do what you were created to do, or be who you were created to be, society will lack what it was supposed to have with YOU in it. That's why society is so off-balance and crazy today, because so many people are not doing what they were created to do—too busy being preoccupied with what everyone else is doing and what everyone else will say.

Do us all a favor and be YOU.

#21 Recognizing Generational Curses

In order to understand generational curses, let's first read about Tracey. For the past two or three years, Tracey has enjoyed going out and having a few drinks. Occasionally, she ends up with a hangover the next day. Just last month, her brother was killed in a car accident because he was driving while drunk. Come to find out her father's brother was an alcoholic and died of kidney failure. After talking to her father about some of the issues he dealt with as a child, she learned that her grandfather used to get drunk and beat her grandmother. Alcoholism was destroying their family. Tracey's family is more than likely operating under a generational curse of alcoholism.

Have you ever heard of the terminology, *generational curses*? Take a moment to examine the habits and circumstances of your parents and their siblings. Then consider the habits and lifestyles of your grandparents and their siblings. Then reach back as far as you are able and recognize the habits and lifestyles of the older generations. Do you notice any patterns from generation to generation? Do you notice some of the same struggles and mishaps? Do you struggle with any of the same issues your parents and their generation deal with? Do you see any of the same negative traits or actions running through your family that have been eating away at and destroying your family for years? If you answered yes to any of these questions, you and your family may be operating under generational curses. In other words, there are certain behaviors or circumstances that are happening to you that happened to your parents and their siblings and their parents and their siblings.

Let's look at Monique's story for an example. Her maternal grandmother was raped at an early age, and so was her mother. Later in life when Monique confided in her mother's two sisters that she had been molested by an older cousin when she was 11, the two sisters (Monique's aunts) told her that they too were molested by an uncle from the ages of about 6 to 12. This is a generational curse—a curse that plagues a family for generations.

A generational curse can live in a family for years and one's life will more than likely be negatively impacted by it unless one takes the time to figure out what the generational patterns are and then declare that it stops with them. One has to recognize it and then say it out loud: "My family is plagued by the generational curse of rape, molestation, and incest. I experienced it; my mother's generation experienced it; her mother's generation experienced it; and possibly further back. I declare today that it ends with me! My children and their children (born or unborn) are protected and blessed and will not have to deal with such a dirty thing!"

After you've made the proclamation, you then walk it out. Be mindful of situations where rape and molestation can occur and live carefully. If and when you have children or if you have younger siblings, don't allow them to spend the night with just anyone. Don't live scared, but don't live carelessly either. Teach your children that no one is to touch them on their private parts or anywhere that makes them uncomfortable and if someone does, they are to come tell you immediately. Teach your children that if someone were to harm them, that person would probably tell them not to tell anyone. Let your children know that's only a fear tactic or a form of manipulation, and that they should scream, kick, holler, run, let the world know—*someone is being inappropriate with me!*

#22 Breaking Generational Curses

Now, sit down with a pen and paper and right down all the negative attributes in your family that you see across generations—the ones you know of at least. You know every family has secrets and closets with skeletons in them. But some of that information has leaked out. Write it down. Write them all, even the ones you are ashamed or embarrassed by. Now, read them out loud. Pray over them and ask God to let the generational curse(s) end with you. Pray that you don't pass them down to your children or your children's children. Pray that you yourself will be delivered from any possible curses on your life and that you will no longer operate under them. Ask God to show you the areas of your life where you may be operating under a curse that you're unaware of. When you discover new areas, call them out, and cast them out. When you become aware and make a declaration of freedom, you release the power it has over you.

#23 Generational Blessings

After calling out the generational curses and denouncing their power, DON'T STOP THERE. Begin to **speak blessings** over your life and your family's life. Call out the things that you want to see in your family, things that may not exist now, but that one day you desire for them to be. Here are some suggestions of what to call out:

- healed relationships
- fathers and mothers married and committed to each other and raising their children together
- a strong desire for education
- financial freedom and no more debt
- the ability to make wise choices throughout life
- deliverance from perverse thoughts and ideas
- deliverance from pornography
- an end to molestation in our family
- deliverance from drug and alcohol abuse
- deliverance from lowly living
- gainful employment throughout the family
- a stable life and disposition

- unselfishness and consideration for others
- healthy homes, healthy minds, and healthy bodies.

In addition to this list, include anything else that comes to mind—call them out one by one and ask God to bring them to pass!

Remember words have power. Give voice to those attributes that you want your family to have and with your voice denounce those things that you want your family to be rid of and then walk in that direction. Do what it takes to live the lifestyle you would want to have and that you would want to pass down to your children.

#24 Write About It

Journal. Write it out. Whatever you may be going through, write about it. Writing provides such a release. "Journaling provides you with a before and after picture." ☺ -Yvonne Sanchez

You can find a nice journal (notebook) at most stores. Spend a little money and pick one up. The written word helps to bring us freedom and deliverance from past hurts. The written word has power because it allows a platform to release the secrets, shame and mistakes that you hold on to. When you see those hurtful areas of your life written out, it helps to accept that those things happened and then to move past them.

#25 The Next 24 Hours

Just for today, don't smoke or drink. Choose to deal with your life sober. Just for today. Smoking, drinking, and popping pills don't take your problems away. The problem is still right there when the high is gone, and sometimes getting high or drunk can complicate a problem depending upon the situation. Instead, be a big girl and choose to face any problems you may have. Work through them. Get a journal and write about them so you can release them. Stop covering them up and dulling your senses with various substances. They will never get solved like that. Talk to someone you trust about whatever it is that's bothering you—a friend, a counselor, an aunt, a professor, a minister. Choose today to be courageous and handle what needs to be handled. Take one day at a time.

#26 Tired of Living?

Are you depressed? Tired of living? Are you suicidal? Let someone know. Tell a trusted adult. Tell someone who loves you so that they can help you or get you the help you need right away. When you have some time, I want you to write down WHY you are suicidal. What happened or didn't happen that makes you want to end your life. Let's get to the root of the issue. Who hurt you? Who didn't love you? Who wasn't there for you? You can't end your life because of what someone else did or didn't do. They are not worth your life.

Or maybe you want to end your life because of something *you* did. You feel guilty or ashamed. No one is without fault. And there is nothing you can do that God cannot forgive and make better. Remember what I said in *#1 Unconditional Love*; there is nothing you can do that will ever make God stop loving you. And if He loves you there is always hope for a bright future.

You are never alone. God is always with you. He loves you and wants the best for you.

#27 What Do I Do with My Life?
Not sure what to do with your life? Don't know your purpose?

What do you love to do? What do you do that brings you joy and betters the people around you as well?

Whatever that thing is, start there! If it doesn't pay the bills, then work for a paycheck, and do *it* after hours until an opportunity presents itself to do *it* for money.

That thing for me is theatre. I absolutely love acting and directing. When I'm on the stage and I can feel the energy of the audience; when I can sway them to tears and bring them to laughter; when I can see their eyes brighten; when I can feel them holding on, waiting for the story to unfold. That's when I am at my highest. That's when I feel like I am on top of the world.

When I was a stay at home mother, I wrote numerous plays, directed and produced them, and often acted in them as well. Unfortunately, I never made much profit. But that was not the ultimate purpose. I currently have a full-time job working at a university, which I truly enjoy and get much fulfillment from, and I do theatre a couple of times a year so that I do not lose my gift. I am committed to keeping my theatre involvement minimal until my youngest son graduates from high school. At that point I will pursue acting with all I've got. I plan to go to Broadway. However, for the time being, I know that acting on that level takes an immense amount of time and my other passion is my family. I love my husband and children and want to be the best wife and mother I can be at this point in my life. My time to be on stage full-time will come!

Whatever you love, do it and give it all you've got. And remember it doesn't have to happen right now but have a plan and go after it!

#28 The Power of Endurance

When you get tired, don't give up. College can get hard. Challenging classes, lack of finances, messy relationships, confusion over your major, difficult professors—all of that and more, can sometimes way you down. But don't give up. Pause. Go home for a visit and get rejuvenated. Breathe, but don't stop moving forward. Press through 'til the end. We don't quit. We don't give up. We don't lose. We win. No matter what it takes—we win! Keep going.

#29 Loving Yourself by Loving Your Life-Source

It's hard to love others if you don't first love yourself. It's hard to love yourself if you don't first love your Creator. It's hard to love your Creator if you don't first understand how much he loves you. God's word says, that he hopes we can get an inkling of *how wide and long and high and deep the love of Christ is* for each of us. By accepting God's love for me, I accept myself more. I gain a better understanding that I was created on purpose and that everything about my being is and was intentional. I am not an accident. My large nose is not an accident. The shape of my body is not an accident. The color of my skin is not an accident. The family I was born into is not an accident. My infectious laughter is not an accident. The God of love made me on purpose *for* a purpose. When I begin to understand that, I begin to understand myself more, accept myself more, and *enjoy* being me more.

If you ignore, disregard, or even hate your Life Source, then how can you love life? I encourage you to get to know God better and get a better understanding of how much he loves you.

#30 The Power of Generosity

Share what you have. It feels so good to give and bless others, even if it's something small. When God sees that you are willing to share what you have been blessed with, He will bless you with more. Remember the open hand policy: if your hand is open, you can freely give *and* freely receive. But if your hand is closed, you'll have a hard time doing either.

I know you're a college student and funds may be limited, but if you buy a coffee for yourself, consider buying one for your study buddy. If you had a great professor or advisor and want them to know it, purchase them a $5 lunch card. There are so many ways you can be generous even on a college budget.

#31 For a Rainy Day

How much did you spend on hair, hair products and upkeep this month?

How much money did you put into savings?

It's important to look good, but don't let your desire to keep up hold you back from what's really important. Maybe your parents lived from check to check, but it is up to you, the next generation, to do better.

It's very important to save some of your income for lots of reasons:

1. It's important to try to have some money left over each month so that you are not living from check to check.
2. It's important to have something set aside so that when you are ready to purchase a car or a home you don't have to borrow

the entire amount of money, instead you can have something to put down on the purchase which will make your monthly payments lower and shorter. Or if you save long enough you can possibly buy the car with cash avoiding loans and interest.

3. It's good to have money set aside in the event of an emergency.

4. You can invest a portion of your savings into stocks and bonds to help your money grow faster.

5. You won't be working all your life more than likely. At some point you will retire, and you will need to have funds set aside for those years of your life. Don't wait until you are middle aged to set aside. Do so now. You can start with setting aside as little as $10 a month and as your income increases, so should your savings!

#32 Buy Now, Pay Later—NOT!

Did you know that a credit card is based on credit? I'm not talking about your bank card that pulls money directly from your bank account that also serves as a debit card. I'm referring to your AmEx card, or MasterCard, or Visa, or any department store for which you have opened an account. It's called spending money you don't really have. It's a loan that you will have to pay back in addition to accrued interest. Are you in debt? Do you owe more than you can pay back?

Stop borrowing so much money. Stop using the credit card. If you don't have enough money to purchase the item, then YOU CANNOT AFFORD IT! So, don't get it. It's called self-control. You have to use it, otherwise you'll be in a dreadful spot and it could take years and lots of discipline to dig your way out of a life of debt.

Don't you get tired of owing people? Do you even use half the items you are still paying for? Do you even know where they are? Make the choice to buy only what you can afford. Then as you mature and prosper you can begin to splurge a little and not have to worry about debt.

#33 Get Back Up
Always get back up after you fall. If we all stayed down after a fall, the whole world would be down.

You may say that you have fallen too much. You're tired of falling and trying to get back up. However, I encourage you that it's easier to get back up and try again than it is to stay down for the remainder of your life. That would be way too much time wasted.

I remember in college, when I surrendered my life to God. One of the commitments I made to him was to be celibate. I was doing so well for months, almost a year. And then, I messed up. I had sex with this guy I had known for years and who had always flirted with me, but nothing had ever happened. I was super lonely that week and happened to run into him. I felt horrible the next day. I had messed up my long stretch of committing my body to celibacy. I had fallen. I went to church that morning. The choir was singing Donnie McClurkin's song, *We Fall Down, But We Get Up*. That song overwhelmed me with God's love and forgiveness. It spoke to me and told me to get up. It told me that God forgave me and that I needed to forgive myself and to pick up where I left off. So, I did. I chose the path of forgiveness and to get up and continue forward.

#34 Don't Keep Falling in the Same Spot

I learned that in this thing called life, there are times that we will fall because we're human, but we can't stay there. We must get up and continue where we left off. I also learned that if we find that we keep falling in the same spot that we may need to change something. In other words, if we keep making the same mistake, then we need to do something differently.

There's a story about a young kid who kept falling off the top bunk. Every night, in the middle of the night, his parents would hear a loud thump and run to the child's room to see her on the floor crying. Her parents decided to watch her sleep one night to see what the problem was—why did she keep falling? They discovered that she fell out of the bunk because she was sleeping right on the edge of the bed, so when she rolled over while dreaming or getting more comfortable, she would fall off. Her parents told her that when she went to bed the next night that she needed to lay all the way against the wall instead of on the edge of the bed; that way when she rolled over, she would still be on the bed.

That's the same with our life. If we are living on the edge, and we make one mistake, we don't give ourselves any other option but to fall. But if we stay away from the edge, it gives us room to make mistakes until we get stronger in that area without having to fall all the way down. If you are trying to be celibate, you can't go to his house at midnight and expect nothing to happen. If you are trying to be sober, you can't go to the liquor store with your friends and think that all you're going to walk out of the store with is a soda. Don't be ridiculous. That's sleeping too close to the edge of the bed. You're setting yourself up to fall. Don't go to his house that late. In fact, don't' go to his place at all. Don't go to the liquor store. If that's your weakness, you have to stay far away from it, otherwise you will eventually fall for it.

#35 Don't Touch!

You are SOME-body; not just *A* body. Stop allowing everybody and anybody to touch your body and enter into your body. Protect your body. It is precious. You are precious. You are somebody. You are not an animal at the petting zoo who stands there for everyone to walk by and pet. Your body is a treasure. Treat it as such.

#36 Enjoy Your Life

Choose to enjoy life. Choose to wake up each day and see it as an opportunity for a fresh start. See it as an opportunity to be blessed *and* to bless someone else. You can walk through each day with your head down, thinking the worst or you can look for the best in each day and enjoy the good that comes. Bad things happen all the time, but you cannot focus on them. Good things happen all the time—that's what you should set your focus on. The more you think good thoughts about yourself, about your life and about others, the better you will feel. A simple prayer that I pray each morning before I roll out of bed is: *Good morning God. Thank you for waking me up today. Bless me today and help me to be a blessing to others. Help me to focus on the good things today and not the bad, no matter what the day holds. Help me to know you and love you a little more today. In Jesus' name, amen.* And then I roll out of bed and do my best to follow suit.

Enjoying life is a choice. It's not just something that happens to you. You have to take control of how you will think and live and choose the best.

#37 Read Something

In addition to your assigned reading for school, read a book on your own. Learn something new. Autobiographies are usually an incredible read. Try a self-help book for self-improvement in an area that you can use help in. Or read a book for pleasure's sake. There's an old saying that goes, *if you want to hide something from a Negro, put it in a book.* If this hideous quote was derived during American slavery it makes perfect sense considering enslaved African

Americans were punished or murdered if caught reading. Being caught with a book in hand was a capital punishment in many slave states. But we are currently in the 21st century. Authors of all genres should no longer be able to hide information from us by putting it in a book. It's a generational curse that numerous Black people still operate under—the detrimental concept that reading is for White people.

Let's make this statement out to be a lie. Choose to read! Knowledge is at your fingertips.

#38 The Library is Free
Visit your campus library to check out a book. Yes, the old school way. Or visit the local bookstore. Pick a book. Bring it home. Turn off the TV and put your phone away. Read. Grow. Expand. There is nothing like flipping through the pages of a book and being exposed to someone else's world or vantage point. Choose to read.

I personally enjoy reading books about my history as a Black woman, also books written by Black women, as well as, books that help me as a woman of God grow mentally, spiritually and emotionally. What kind of books do you enjoy reading?

#39 Do You Know Your History?

Know your history. Know the real history of America—not just what they taught you in grade school. Read history from a broader perspective. The danger in not knowing your history is that it can be repeated. Knowledge brings wisdom. Wisdom brings direction. Direction brings progress.

I'll give you an example of the dangers of not knowing history. Africans and their descendants were dehumanized and enslaved under chattel slavery in America. Learning to read was outlawed for an enslaved African. In fact, on many plantations, if caught trying to read, one would undergo physical and psychological abuse at the hand of the slaveholder or overseer. In some states, it was a capital offense, punishable by death. Slave holders were opposed to their "slaves" being educated because they knew it would empower them and ultimately undermine the slaveholder's authority. Knowing just that bit of history, makes me hungry for education—understanding what it can do for my life and the doors it can open. But if I didn't know that part of history, and I had friends who said dumb things like *reading is for white people* or *school is dumb* I may, like them, de-value education and not partake in it. This would then allow history to repeat itself, but without the slaveholder having to enforce it.

School is cool.

Although school is important, I understand that all professors aren't great professors and not all assignments are relevant. However, choose to do well in school despite the rigmarole. When a lecture is biased, challenge it. When the instructor is teaching with a lopsided perspective, offer another perspective. However, you can't offer another perspective if you haven't taken responsibility for your own education. Do some reading on your own. Find books that interest you. Or do it the old-fashioned way and ask the librarian for assistance. Learning is not confined to the classroom.

Know your history. Don't allow the ugliness of yesterday to repeat itself today.

#40 What Slavery Called Us

Do you know who Frederick Douglass is? He was an enslaved African-American during American slavery in the 1800's. He was brutally treated and dehumanized. He looked for ways to gain his freedom. Finally, after much turmoil and struggle, his strong desire became his reality. He was able to escape the perils of the South to reside in the North and was no longer a "slave" but a freeman.

He wrote an autobiography, *Narrative of the Life of Frederick Douglass, an American Slave*, explaining his experiences and the horrors of slavery. He told of one such story about a slave master who would call his female slaves—*black b**ches*.

Wow, it's remarkable how times have changed. Instead of the white slave owner, through an institutional system of oppression and degradation, calling us b**ches, African Americans call ourselves that and dance to the beat of the b**ch lyrical music. SMH

Are you aware that the slave master, a little over 100 years ago, called your great-great-grandmother a b**ch? Then he'd beat her. Then he'd have his way with her. Then he'd leave her there until the next time he wanted some.

If you are dating the "slave master" just in different skin and clothing, then wake up. Don't allow history to keep repeating itself. You have the power to stop this generational curse. You have a choice; your great-great-grandmother did not.

#41 What We Call Ourselves

It breaks my heart when I hear a woman call another woman a b**ch. And not just any woman, not even her enemy, but her friend, or her own self. Or what about when a mother calls her own daughter a b**ch? That hurts. You may not think this to be that big of a deal, however considering history (see #40) and considering what the word means, it seems destructive to me. If words have power, then what do I have to gain by calling my friends "female dogs" or in other words "unpleasant" or "malicious?" I want to speak life into my own life and into the lives of my friends and daughters. I love when I go visit my cousins or get on the phone with my sister and they say, *hello Love.* I love when they call me *Love.* It fills me with such joy and makes me feel loved. When a friend calls me b**ch, I know she doesn't mean any harm, but it definitely doesn't give me any life.

#42 Woman Up!

You have no control over your childhood and things that happened to you back then. Whether you were neglected, molested, abused, or forgotten—you had no control. However, you can't keep blaming your childhood for what is going on in your life now. You have to stop placing the blame and take responsibility of your life. You can't control what happened to you, but you can control what you do with the rest of your life. You have to stop blaming your current situation on what your dad did. You have to stop blaming your mistakes on your dad's absence. You have to stop placing the blame for your misfortune on what your mother did or didn't do. They probably did the best they knew to do.

Your life is in your hands now. Forgive them. Make good choices and your life will turn around for the better.

#43 Don't Be a Thermometer

It is very important to know who you are. You should have a strong sense of self. Know your likes, your dislikes, what brings you joy, what brings you pain. Know your musts and your must-nots, what is good for you and what is wrong for you, and more. If you do not know who you are you will be like a chameleon—you change to fit into whatever environment you are in, instead of being *you*, wherever you are.

How can you avoid this constant changing to fit into

different spaces? How do you get to know yourself and have a strong identity? If you are looking for your identity through your friends, or social media, or your major, or your job, or intimate relationships, or through clothes and material things, or through music, or reality shows, or through drinking or indulging in various drugs—you'll never, **ever** find yourself. In fact, you'll be going farther away from ever discovering who you really are. Stop looking for yourself outside and come on inside. Get quiet, be still, and spend time alone with you. Take time to talk to God and ask Him to help you find your identity. After all, God is your Creator. It makes sense that your Creator would know the most about you and could help you discover you.

#44 Emotions Gone Wild

Now let's look at your emotions. Are they all over the place? Mine were. I allowed what happened to me throughout the day and my interactions with others to dictate my emotions. Which meant my emotions were wild? They were all over the place. I could be angry, happy, sad, excited, and depressed all within one day. And it was all contingent upon external interactions.

I decided one day I didn't want to live like that

anymore. I wanted to be emotionally stable. I wanted to be happy no matter what was thrown at me. I learned that I was the only one who could make that change in my life. My parents couldn't do it for me. My older brothers and sisters couldn't do it for me. The pastor couldn't do it for me. My friends couldn't do it for me. Only I could do it for myself. I wanted better so I chose to respond better. I chose to not allow people and life's circumstances to control me. I chose stability. If you struggle with emotional instability, I encourage you to choose better as well.

#45 The Power of Stability

It's important to be stable, both mentally and emotionally. You can't allow your thoughts to run wild. You can't follow every emotion that you feel. You must learn how to use self-control and shut some thoughts and emotions down. If not, you will have a crazy and unstable life. I used to let whatever thought that popped into my head have its way. I didn't realize I could tell a thought to leave and then replace it with a positive thought.

Just think about all the ridiculous thoughts that invade your mind, for example:

- I hate my family

- I hate my life
- I wish I could be her
- I hate school
- I am the dumbest person in this classroom
- I'll never graduate

If you allow those thoughts to remain, they can lead to some detrimental circumstances if you don't grab them and get them out as soon as they enter. Doing so is not easy at first. It's like trying to squeeze a black head on your nose. It hurts and it seems impossible. However, your brain is a muscle that can be exercised and become stronger and healthier. Think of your biceps—if you do arm curls with 10lb weights, over time, that muscle will get stronger and look more toned. Eventually though, ten pounds will be too easy, and you will have to increase the weight to 15lbs in order to keep getting results.

The same is true for your mind—when harmful thoughts (harmful for you and others) enter your mind it's important to say, "No, I don't have to think that." Stop the thought and then replace it with a positive thought. Here are positive thoughts to replace the ridiculous thoughts from above:

- I am thankful for my family no matter how dysfunctional we can be

- I am thankful for my life and I will live it to the fullest
- I am glad God made me. I will choose to enjoy my life and appreciate who I am.
- I am grateful that I am in school. I realize it's a privilege to receive a higher education
- I am intelligent and I will do my best
- I'm excited about graduating

After you put this into practice, replacing negative thoughts with positive ones, over time it will become easier to do—just as lifting the 10lb weight becomes easier over time. Your life will improve as well. After all, our thoughts become our actions, our actions our habits, and our habits our lifestyle. So, practice thinking good thoughts. Take ownership of them and make the best of them.

#46 Read the Directions

If you purchase a piece of furniture, say from IKEA, you need to read the directions in order to put it together properly—right? If you do not read the directions before attempting to assemble the parts you may put some things together wrong, or leave some pieces out altogether, and more than likely the piece of furniture will be raggedy or even fall apart after time has passed because the directions weren't followed. The same goes for your life. If you are trying to put the pieces of your life together without looking at the Instructions for Life, i.e. The Creator's Manual, a.k.a. The Bible, you too will not be put together properly and could possibly one day fall apart.

God's Word is full of directions and instructions for everyday living. If you read it and commit yourself to applying what you read, you will grow, you will change, and your life will be better. I didn't say that you would be without problems. But you will gain the wisdom and strength necessary to go *through* your challenging situations with peace and come out better and stronger. Notice the emphasis on "through." You don't have to live with the problem—God is able to help you come out of the problem. And when God delivers you from something, you come out wiser, stronger, and better.

One of my favorite scriptures is 1 John 4:18. It reads, "There is no fear in love. But perfect love drives out fear, because fear has to do with torment. The one who fears is not made perfect in love." Another version states that "fear is crippling." It keeps you from moving forward. It keeps you stuck. My experiences with fear throughout my life are exactly that—it cripples me. The scripture says that love drives out fear. And if you read a few verses ahead of verse 18 it states that "God is love." Therefore, the closer you get to God (or to love), the less presence and power fear has in your life—the less fear can torment you or cripple you. That's so good!

Another favorite scripture of mine is Philippians 4:6-7. It reads, "Do not worry about anything; instead, pray about everything. Tell God what you need and thank him for all he has done. Then you will experience God's peace which exceeds anything we can understand. His peace will guard your hearts and minds as you live in Christ Jesus." It's important to read this verse like a list of detailed instructions on what to do to be at peace, or at ease—without anxiety. If I could, for a minute, restructure the scripture for you, so that you can see more easily what to do when you are lacking peace:

1. Stop worrying
2. Instead, pray about whatever it is that is bothering you
3. During your prayer, talk to God about what you need
4. While you're still praying, thank him for everything you can think to thank him for
5. Sit and wait for his peace to overwhelm you

6. Live a life that is in line with what Jesus would desire for you. In other words, be obedient

If you just breezed through the scripture and didn't pay attention to what exactly it explains to do to require peace, you will miss all the simple steps it lays out. And I think sometimes we neglect step 6, or we don't realize the significance of it. We can't keep living life our own way, living life by our own rules, and expect to get God's results. If we want to have the peace, joy, prosperity, blessings, and health that God promises throughout his word, then we have to be willing to do things his way. We must choose to be obedient. I encourage you today to choose obedience. It's not always easy, but it's worth it. You won't always get it right the first time, but with practice and time, obedience becomes easier. And you can ask God to help you to be obedient. Yes, ask for his help.

And one thing extra that I've learned along the way is that it's easier to be obedient to Jesus if you love him. So, in addition to asking God to give you the desire to be obedient, ask him to help you to LOVE him with all your heart, mind, soul and strength. When you love someone and you understand how much they love you, it's easier to follow them.

#47 Godly Obedience

Sometimes we want a blessed life, but we don't want to do what it takes to have a blessed life. We do things our way but still expect God's results. If you are a Christian, then doing things your way and expecting God's results, will not work. We must be obedient if we want God to turn things around for us and bless us abundantly. We can't continue to wake up each morning and give God the finger and then expect him to bless us. What do I mean by give God the finger? Well, that means that you profess to be a believer, a Christian, but your lifestyle says differently.

Pause and take a good look at your lifestyle, your day-to-day thoughts, your actions and in-actions. Do they honor God? Do they make him look good? Or do your thoughts and actions scream *f**k you God*?

God's word clearly states, if you obey me, I will bless you, but if you disobey me, then I will curse you. Is your life blessed or cursed? Is it on the up-and-up or is it jacked up?

But how will you know if you are obedient or disobedient if you don't get into the word of God to find out how it says to live your life? You can't just go off what your pastor or your parents say for the rest of your life. That's for babies. It's time to grow up and study God's word on your own. Not sure how to study the Bible? Do an internet search like you would everything else— "how to study the Bible".

One of the ways I read the Bible that is extremely helpful for me is to think of an issue or topic that I am currently dealing with or something that comes up in my life often, such as "anger" or "insecurity." Then I go to the internet and search for "scriptures on anger." Immediately, numerous verses on that topic will come up. Then I pick one or two of those scriptures to focus on for the day. After reading them, I write them down. Then I pick out key words in the scripture and search for their definition and write the definition down. Even if I know what the word means already, I will still look it up and write it down. Doing so, adds so much depth to the words and therefore to the scripture, making it that much more understandable, impactful, and applicable.

Finally, I ask God to help me to apply what I just read. What is the point of reading and studying scripture if you have no intent on applying it? Choose to apply God's word and see how it changes your life!

#48 Not Your Story

Please don't allow this to be your story. If any part of the scenario below resembles your experience, then stop what you're doing and change the direction you're headed in...

...You're finally out of your parents' home! Yes! You should be studying but last night you went out and got wasted. Tonight, you plan on getting high with the crew. Tomorrow you're going to Forever 21 to pick up that hot outfit for the club. You're probably gonna leave the club with what's-his-name. The two of you will get high and do it. Then the following night you hook up with your steady guy and go to the movies and dinner and then come back to your dorm and do it, even though your roommate is in the bed right next to you. Your grades start slipping. You find out that you're pregnant, and you think it's your boyfriend's, but you're not sure. You can't drop out of school and you can't tell your parents, so you get an abortion. You end up depressed because you aborted your baby and to deal with the depression you start smoking more...

...Don't let any part of this be your story.

You have the power to change the direction your life

is headed in if it's going the wrong way. Take a moment and reflect on your life and the direction its going in. If any part of it seems questionable, figure out what you can do differently in order to create better results. You may not have had the power over your past, as a child, but you are in college now and it's time to start taking charge of your life and making good choices. A series of good choices will lead to a good life. The opposite is true as well: a series of bad choices will lead to a bad life. If you choose to make good choices, please be aware that bad things will still occur, but ultimately your life will be good. The opposite is true as well. I hope you make the right choice.

#49 Something My Mom Told Me

My mother once told me, "You are so beautiful, both inside *and* out; I can't determine which one is more beautiful." I'll never forget that. ☺

Make sure you spend as much time (or more) beautifying your character—who you are as a person, as you do in the mirror perfecting your attire, make-up, and hair. Your character matters.

#50 Master Manipulator

When you don't get your way, how do you react? Do

you pout? Do you cry? Get angry? Stop talking to the opposing individual? Walk out? Get upset and give someone a piece of your mind? These are all examples of manipulation—a way to control the situation to get things to turn in your favor. I used to do all the above. I never thought of it as manipulation. I just figured if I didn't get my way, it was only natural, normal, and acceptable for me to react as such. I didn't realize I was behaving like a child. I had to learn that not everything is going to go my way all the time. I had to learn to be flexible and willing to give up control. I had to make the choice to say, it's okay that it didn't turn out like I had planned, this other way will be fine, and I will enjoy it as well.

If you respond in any of the ways previously mentioned, then it's possible that you are a manipulator. Manipulators are hard to be in relationship with because one must walk on eggshells around them to keep them happy. No one wants to be around someone that you have to be so delicate with as not to anger them. Choose to recognize any patterns of manipulation you may have, then choose to not operate under them. Ask friends and family to hold you accountable. It may be hard to change, but it is possible, and it is worth it! The people in your life will appreciate it!

#51 No More Excuses

If your life is pathetic, stop blaming everyone else. Stop giving piss poor excuses for the disarray in your life, such as... "I didn't have a daddy" or "My momma didn't teach me" or "My mother doesn't care" or "Nobody loves me" or "She did it, so why can't I?" Ask yourself *did it work for her?* If not, what makes you think it will turn out better for you? Stop with all the excuses. Those excuses were acceptable when you were younger. You were given the benefit of the doubt. But you are older now. It's time to take responsibility for your life. Act like you have some sense. You know better, so do better, and then you will have better.

Did you know that everyone is born with the innate ability to distinguish right from wrong? So whether someone taught you or not—deep down inside you know what's best. You know what a good choice is, and you know what a poor choice is. It's up to you to choose to acknowledge and respond to that innate morality.

#52 Porn is Detrimental to Your Being

Stop watching pornography. Yes, it may be enticing and exhilarating but it's poisonous to your mind, heart, and spirit. It lures you in, right? You catch one glimpse of it and your body starts tingling. That tingle doesn't mean "give me more!" That tingle is an indication that if you don't turn it off NOW, then you are in danger of getting trapped. I strongly encourage you to turn it off. Delete your sources from your phone or computer. Stop going to Adult Stores. Just stop. If you don't stop, you'll always want more. It's a desire that can never be satisfied. It has a way of pulling you in and trapping you. It may start off as an innocent viewing, but it can lead to a toxic lifestyle. It has a way of impacting your entire life. For example, it can cause you to be physically unfulfilled during sex due to yearnings for fictitious, pornographic situations you've seen.

What if that was your little sister or daughter in the video or magazine? What if that was your little brother or son? Would that be okay with you? ... If you answered "yes" to either question—you have issues. Get some help. Get some counseling.

Did you know that for men and women to perform in those videos, the majority of them are on a chemical substance? They have to alter their state of mind and kill their brain cells in order to participate in the video. Don't you care about their well-being? You should.

If absorbing pornography is a habit of yours and you want to stop or you know you *need* to stop but you don't know how, here's a tip. I've found that the best way to stop a bad habit is to start a new healthy habit to replace it with. Think of something you enjoy doing or something you've been wanting to try, like painting or yoga. Spend your time doing those things and you will have less time to put into poisoning your mind and attributing to the detriment of others. Take control of your actions and your mind—only you can. And you're very capable of doing so.

#53 Slow Down and Enjoy the Ride

Patience. It's good to be patient. If you are an anxious individual, that can lead to a stressful life, a life in which you don't know how to relax and enjoy the moment. Stress is a form of dis-ease in your spirit and being. Our spirit is connected to our physical body. *Dis-ease* within our spirit can lead to *disease* in our physical body. I'm not saying that all dis-ease turns into a disease, but many stresses in our life manifest themselves in our flesh and we can wind up with heart failure, low blood flow, obesity, high blood pressure, depression, and more. Learn to pause and take a slow deep breath. Stretch. Relax. Forgive.

If things don't happen when you want them to happen, it's not the end of the world. If people don't do what you want them to do, it's not the end of the world. Go easy on people, and life will go easier on you. And don't be so hard on yourself. Breathe. Relax. Forgive. Be patient. Enjoy the journey. Enjoy the journey to finish school. Enjoy the journey to finding the right relationship. Enjoy the journey to landing the ideal career. Enjoy the journey to becoming a better version of yourself. Enjoy the journey of learning to be a better friend. Enjoy life.

Learn to be thankful and not complain. Don't try to force something that maybe shouldn't happen right now. Choose patience. An old saying that stands the test of time is *good things come to those who wait.*

#54 Set Goals

Always set goals for your life. Then when you reach a goal, pause, celebrate, and enjoy it; be in the moment for however long the moment lasts. When you reach a goal, always set another one. Aspire to do bigger and better things that will make the world a brighter and healthier place. Write your goals down. Look at them every once in a while. Gauge your progress. Research what you need to do to reach your goal. Inquire from those who have done what you want to do. Push. Work. Sweat. Wait. Try. Press. Endure. Enjoy.

An example of setting a goal and reaching it in my own life, was setting a goal to finish this book and get it in your hands. Towards the end I learned to write deadlines for each stage of completion on a sticky note and stick it in a place that I would see it every day. And once I accomplished that stage, I'd write a new sticky note with a new deadline. There were times where nothing was being done because life got in the way. My children were active, my job got overwhelming, my father passed away, I was in grad school, my oldest sister passed away, my mother needed my help, and more… but I knew I had to finish. Although life delayed me from reaching my goal it also allowed me to write a better book because I learned something through all those life challenges which enhanced the content of this book. So, don't look at all roadblocks as blockage but possibly as a channel to gain something new to help to further develop the end-goal. Set your goal, keep it before you, allow life to mold and shape it, and never give up until you reach it!

#55 Finish Strong
Finish strong. Whatever you start, finish and finish

strong.

I wrote this manual years before I rewrote it which was a long time before getting it published. God put it in my heart in 2011, and it seemed like I would never finish it. But it never left my spirit to complete it because I knew I wanted you to read it and that some part of it would have an impact on your life and help you to make better choices for a better life. So, I pushed and worked and waited and pressed and endured. And finally, it's in your hands. I finished!

Take the time to review it. Reflect on it. Write your thoughts down on it. Reread it. And please, share it.

Whatever you have in your heart to do, start it and finish it. It will be worth it!

PART 2
RELATIONSHIPS & STICKY SITUATIONS

#56 Fatherless Does Not Equal Hopeless

Fatherless is NOT synonymous with hopeless. Just because you may not have a father in your life, whether you never knew him, whether he left your mommy when you were 3 years old, whether he came around on birthdays and holidays only, or some other unfortunate circumstance, that doesn't mean you are hopeless. In fact, it doesn't have to mean you are without a father either. If you look up "fatherless" in the dictionary it says, *not having a living father* or *not having a known or legally responsible father*. But if you look up "fatherless" in God's word, he tells you that he's a father to the fatherless. He was prepared. He knew some dads would be missing and make stupid choices to not be in their children's lives. If this is your situation, God's got you.

Remember, you have your entire life in front of you. Live it to the fullest and don't allow fatherlessness to be an excuse for hopelessness or for making stupid choices. Instead, choose to let God fill the void and make choices that will help your life to be better and not worse. It's your life—not your father's—so make the best of it!

#57 Dating Should Be Fun

Enjoy dating. Date lots of people. You don't have to date exclusively. Try lots of new things and adventures. Movies and dinner are cool, but there's so many other things you can do with your date. Try the following:

- hiking
- having a picnic
- swimming
- boating
- kayaking
- fishing
- playing sand volleyball (with other friends)
- playing tag football (with other friends)
- painting
- walking and enjoying scenery
- making something together

I'm sure there are plenty more ideas. If you think of any, write them down, that way next time you go on a date, you have a list of ideas to pull from. Enjoy! Have fun! Make good choices.

#58 If You Were Molested

Were you molested as a child? I've heard it said, that if a child is molested, it can do one of two things to the child:

1. The child shuts down sexually, or
2. They can become hypersexual.

Pertaining to the first, if a child shuts down sexually, as an adult they are often marked "asexual" which can reveal itself through one looking homely, wearing clothing and hairstyles that are extremely unattractive to keep the opposite sex at bay. They don't want any involvement with sex or even a sexual touch. It makes them feel dirty, uncomfortable, and ashamed. They miss out on the enjoyment of being created as a sexual being with sexual desires.

The other possible outcome of being molested is that the child becomes very sexually aware, often/even overtly sexual. They see everything through a sexualized lens. This can be dangerous if not properly handled, and as soon as possible. Any relationship, whether with a male or female, can become entangled in sex and sexual acts from an early age. Usually sex or something sexual will always be involved in most of their relationships. They can become overly thirsty for sex and often perverted in their ways.

In both possible outcomes, whether the individual is inclined to either asexuality or hyper-sexuality, a sexual touch or act can sometimes trigger an awkward, disgusting, and evasive feeling—even with a trusted partner or with-in a long-term relationship. If the underlying causes of triggers are not properly handled/addressed, they can corrode a healthy relationship, even a marriage. Both asexuality and hypersexuality, as a result of being molested, can lead to feelings of inadequacy, unworthiness, shame, guilt, and displeasure with life. If this has happened to you, you don't have to live with this baggage for the rest of your life. If you've been molested—get help. Get good help. Start with your mentor? Don't have a mentor, start with an older woman you love and trust. Visit the counseling center at your school. Does your church have a counseling ministry? If not, find out if your friend's church has one. It's never too late to seek help. Don't run from the healing because of fear. Fear is a nasty barrier to a good life. Instead, run for your life. It's worth the challenge and the pain you may have to experience when unloading baggage. You want to be the best you can possibly be. So, do not be afraid to get help. Now. Not later. Of course, there are other harmful outcomes that can stem from being molested other than becoming hypersexual or asexual. However, molestation more than likely affected you in some way; please don't ignore the effects. If it is never brought up and dealt with, it could leave you scarred for the rest of your life and infect all of your relationships. My desire is for you to be healed from all possible effects of this wretched thing so that you can be who God created you to be!

Others have been where you are—many have received healing, many have not. I hope you choose to be healed.

#59 Bad Little Girl

Did someone—your mother, your auntie, or your cousin, call you "bad" when you were little? They may have said something like, *that's a bad little girl* or *that little girl is just bad*. I want to tell you today that you were not bad as a child. You were a child and children behave like children. But that doesn't make you *bad*. You are not *bad*. God made you well. He wasn't having a bad day when He created you.

Do you know where that came from—when Black

parents call their child bad? This degradation of one's own child is rooted in American slavery. When a slave owner wanted to purchase a young slave and ultimately separate the family, tearing mother from child, the mother would cry out, *No, no sir you don't want this child here. This child is bad*. She would say that in hopes that the slave owner would skip over her child when pursuing new "property." Property—exactly. Property or goods can be "bad" or of no value, but not people. People can make bad choices, but they themselves are not bad. Slaves adopted the mentality that they were just property and in so doing referred to their offspring as bad or damaged goods to protect them. Generations later, Black parents are still saying, *my child is bad.* Only now those words don't protect; they tear down. And more often than not, that kid grows up to behave "bad"—simply living up to what mommy called them. If someone in your family, or a teacher possibly, called you bad, it is not true. You are not bad. You may make bad choices, but that can change. You were for created for greatness!

#60 How to Say NO
Come on babe, just let me…yea, right there…it'll feel so good… How do you say NO when you like a guy and you feel the pressure to say yes? Below are some

ways to help you say NO... One way to help you say NO is to *play the movie to the end*. In other words, fast forward the situation in your mind to the end of the night or maybe even to the end of the relationship. What are the likely results? Be honest with yourself. Okay, for example, this is what's happening... You're with him in his car. He's driving you home from the party. He looks so damn fine. The plan is for him to drop you off at your apartment and keep going, but when he pulls up in front of your building, he asks you, "Do you want me to walk you inside?" This is the point where you need to **play the movie to the end** in your mind really quickly: *I don't want to have sex with him, but if he walks me to my door, he's going to reach in for a kiss and it's going to feel really good and I'm probably going to get wet. Hell, I'm wet now just thinking about it. Then after the kiss (and his lips are so freakin' juicy), he's probably going to want to come inside my apartment and I'm not going to be able to resist and once he comes in, it's over. It's going down for sure. And then tomorrow, I could wake up with an STD or simply with another guy to add to my list that I f**ked and that I had no relationship with and then I'll feel guilty. The End.*

Is that what you want to happen? Is it worth it? Don't

make up a happily ever after ending, or even an *it doesn't matter if we just f**k* ending. This is not a fairytale we are talking about here. This is your life. Keep it real. Think it through, thoroughly. If the ending looks bleak, and it ends up just like the last situation then don't do it. It's not worth it.

Another idea is to simply have the courage to let the word NO come out of your mouth, but you have to mean it. I mean, you have to back it up with your actions. Don't say NO at noon, over the phone, but then when he calls you at 2 in the morning to come "kick it" you put on your shoes and go. Really? Don't be an idiot. Or, don't say NO, but then wear the most revealing outfit you can possibly find on your next date—you are only tempting yourself and him. (And no, I'm not saying you are responsible if he tries to take advantage of you because of what you chose to wear. I'm simply referring to the fact that certain clothing can make you *and your date* even more horny and make it harder for you to keep your word.) Also, don't say NO, and then get naked with him and say *we are only gonna cuddle*. Yeah right. Don't put yourself up to that kind of temptation.

Also, try wearing granny panties—that way, when he tries to pull your skirt up or unzip your pants, you will be determined not to let him see because you refuse to be embarrassed.

Another simple tool is to remind yourself that your body is a gift not to be toyed with by every interested, temporary admirer.

When trying to say NO, consider the obvious but often forgotten show-stoppers—STDs! The fear of contracting Herpes, Gonorrhea, Syphilis, HIV, and other STDs should always be at the forefront of your mind. You never know what he or she is carrying. They may not know either. It may be worth noting that just because you can't see the STD doesn't mean it doesn't exist. Often, men can carry sexually transmitted diseases and never experience any symptoms. He could pass it to you and not even know that he has it. Or worse, he could know about it and not care about spreading it. We often think that *things like that will never happen to me,* but *why not me*?

Finally, think about your heart. Yes, I know he can wear a condom to protect you from unwanted pregnancies and STDs, but a condom can't protect you from a broken heart.

#61 Establish Boundaries

When I was growing up, we had lines. Barriers. There were just some lines we didn't cross. There were some things we just didn't do. We knew better. It seems like today's mindset is, *if you think it, you do it. If it will make you feel good, it's all good. No lines. Just do what you want to do, and who cares about the consequences, right?* Wrong.

Hopefully you do care and you do realize that all your choices have consequences. Life is all about making choices—good ones and bad ones. Good choices can lead to good things and bad choices can lead to bad things. Of course, good and bad can happen in anyone's life. Ultimately a series of good choices will lead to a good life and vice versa. There should be some things you just are NOT going to do. Why? Because you know better. Whether your friends participate in certain activities or not, or whether society has made something seem normal or acceptable, doesn't make it good for you. Choices are accompanied with consequences. Your freedom doesn't come from living however you want to live and doing whatever comes to mind. No, your freedom comes from living a life you can be proud of, a life that God can smile on—that's when you feel free to live life to the fullest and become all you were created to be! When God smiles on your life, when he approves of your choices, and when your choices honor him, then he can trust you and bless you with even more greatness!

#62 The Cycle

You keep doing things the same way expecting a different outcome. I'll say that again in another way...

- You keep having sex with random individuals and then wonder why you're no longer together after a few short dates
- You keep showing up to work late and wondering why you are not getting promoted or even worse, wondering why you got fired
- You keep spending money you don't have and wondering why you are in so much debt
- You keep cussing friends and family out who piss you off and wonder why you have so many enemies
- You keep eating unhealthy food and barely getting in any exercise and then wonder why your dress size is increasing and why you're always lethargic
- You rarely clean up after yourself and wonder why you live in a dump

- You constantly fall asleep in class and wonder why your GPA is slipping

Do you want different results? Then change what you do. Make better choices. If not, you can get trapped in a viscous cycle of bad choices and bad results, bad choices and bad results, bad choices and bad results... In order to escape the negative cycle, you have to substitute your bad choices with good ones, healthy ones, positive ones, and so on.

#63 Can Sex Fill the Void Where Love Should be?

Have you ever thought that having sex will make you feel loved? It won't. Maybe during the act of sex, you are able to feel the intimacy and closeness with that person to the extent that it feels like love, but it's not. Sex is not love and love is not sex. Don't get them twisted, otherwise you could wind up feeling further from love the more sex you have.

#64 Holding Grudges

It may have happened three years ago or even six months ago, but you are still holding on to it and playing what happened over and over again in your mind—keeping the anger fresh and alive. Holding on to it is not healthy.

How do you solve conflict between you and a friend or family member? Do you lash out and seek after revenge? Do you hate on her? Do you hold it against him and choose never to talk to him again? If so, your ways are childish. You are moving into adulthood now. It's time to handle things in a more mature way. You don't have to have an argument every time someone does you wrong. You can let some things go and recognize that that person is human, just like you are, and that they will make mistakes, just like you do. You don't have to take revenge; that only escalates the situation. Choose to be the bigger person and walk away, then come back and deal with it at the right time and in a calm manner. Even go as far as to recognize your potential faults in the situation. Remember, we are not always innocent. Forgive someone, because there will come a time when you need forgiveness. Just because you forgive someone does not mean you have to be in relationship with them. Depending upon how they hurt you, you can forgive them and decide that the relationship is not healthy for you, but you can still choose to be cordial to that person when you see them. You can choose to move on but move on gracefully. If you choose to stay, let the issue go, and allow the relationship to grow. Sometimes working through tough situations with a friend can make the relationship better and stronger!

#65 To: A Sexual Assault Victim

Has anyone ever sexually assaulted you? How did you feel afterwards? How have you felt since? Dirty? Defeated? Lifeless? Stupid? Ugly? Angry? Evil? Nasty? Enraged? Worthless? Panicked? Sex-Craved? Asexual? Awkward? You've possibly felt all these things and more. If you haven't already, please tell someone who you trust what happened to you. Don't believe the lie that you must keep it a secret. Secrets have a way of haunting you and tormenting you. Secrets are like words and thoughts locked inside of a dungeon that need to be freed. Once the secret has been revealed in a safe space and in the right setting, little by little, it loses its ability to haunt and control you. That's when the healing process begins. Yes, healing is possible! Remember, words have power. Locked up words that need to be released can have the wrong type of power over your thoughts. Tell someone you trust and let what happened to you out.

Once you have told someone you trust, then seek counseling. Take the necessary steps to be free from the painful past. You can be free from this entanglement with pain, but you have to go *through* the pain to *come out* of the pain. I know that may sound scary to you, but your healing is on the other side of the pain. And you can do what it takes to be free. You are able. Just get help. If you don't have insurance to cover counseling, then spend your expendable money. It's worth it. It's more important than any clothing item or hair product you would purchase.

If you don't get help to gain freedom from this horrible evil, it can control the rest of your life. It will affect your relationships with your family, friends, and significant other(s). If you don't get help you will always be a victim. It is exhausting to be in relationship with people who possess a victim mentality. Some attributes of someone with a victim mentality are:

- they are always looking for others to make them happy
- they are manipulative
- they do not trust others
- they are always expecting someone to hurt them and ready to take revenge
- they can be very insecure and think lowly of themselves

- they want others to always apologize to them for any minor or major injustice towards them

If you have been sexually assaulted and any of the aforementioned attributes describe you, get help now. Get help, so that you can have healthy, whole relationships, not just with others, but with yourself especially. Learn to like yourself. Love yourself. Be the best you can be every day. Freedom from your past is available, go after it!

You may also want to strongly consider filing a police report so that the predator can be locked up.

#66 The Power of Forgiveness

You've heard it before, *let it go. Forgive and move on.* However, your response may be, *but you just don't understand, (name of person) hurt me so bad, it's too hard to forgive.* Actually, it is more difficult to live with unforgiveness and bitterness, than it is to forgive. Bitterness eats away at your life and your joy. It destroys you from the inside out when you hold on to what someone did to hurt you. We often replay in our minds what the person did and how much disdain we have for that person—over and over again. The more you rehearse how they hurt you, the angrier you become. The more you remind yourself of the reasons why you dislike or even hate that person, the more bitterness you begin to harbor. It is true, you probably do have a valid reason to be angry at them, but you do not have to hate them. Why not? We all need a pass at times. Remember, you too are capable of hurting someone and you probably have before in the past. You are human.

Humans hurt other humans, whether intentionally or not. We can't go on hating everyone who hurts us otherwise we will end up with no one to love. Everyone you are in relationship with will hurt you at some point. Everyone. I'm not recommending you must remain in relationship with everyone, but you can and should forgive everyone. You've heard it said, *not forgiving someone is like drinking poison and expecting the other person to die from it.* But really, not forgiving hurts you more than it hurts the other person.

Are you so special that no one should hurt you? We live in an imperfect world. Hurt is going to happen. Set your mind that you will be **ready to forgive** anyone who harms you. Set your mind to live free of bitterness. Program your mind to live free of holding on to the people who harmed you and free from reminding yourself of that hurt and remaining angry at them. That's too much weight to carry around. We tend to repeatedly replay in our minds how they misused us, so that the next time we see them we can chew them out and be able to give them a laundry list of all the ways they hurt us. I know, I have tormented myself in that way many a times, thinking I can't wait to see them and tell them all the horrible things they did to me and then give them a piece of my mind. We even have a script of how we are going to cuss them out. DON'T DO THAT! Take it from me, that's extra baggage that you don't need to carry. That is space in your mind and heart that you can use for more constructive things. Choose freedom. Choose forgiveness. If you say, "I can't" then my response is "that's your choice." I encourage you to choose better.

#67 Dating Should Be a Learning Experience

The person you are dating now, may not be the person you are with next year, or even next month for that matter. Try not to get so caught up in one person, especially at such a young age. Dating should be a learning experience not a life-draining one. Sometimes, we can get so connected and "in love" with that one person and practically give our life over to them which is not healthy. Then when a break-up occurs, we feel like life is over. Dating doesn't have to be that type of experience.

Use dating as a learning tool. As you date and get to know more people, learn what like and what you don't like. Learn what you will deal with and what are deal-breakers for you in a relationship. That way as you start to think about marriage, later on in life, you will have a better idea of what type of person you want to marry. Remember though that all people are human—no one is perfect. There will be things about people that you will just have to accept if you want the relationship to last. And remember you are not perfect either, so there will be some things about you, that your partner will have to accept as well. It goes both ways.

If the relationship you are in right now does not last, it's okay. It's not the end of the world. Move on. Count it as a learning experience. What did you do well in that relationship? What could you have done better? What qualities did you acquire from the relationship? What negative things did you pick up that you can dump? Learn and grow and keep it moving.

#68 Stop Being a Victim

Do you think everyone is out to hurt you? Do you look at ever situation as if someone was intentionally trying to harm you? Do you see everything from a negative vantage point? If so, it's possible that you have a victim mentality.

Do you think you are the only person in life who has been stepped on? Trampled over? Neglected? You are not. Get over yourself. You don't have to be a victim your whole life and expect people to feel sorry for you and always need someone to apologize to you. Everyone has been hurt. Everyone has been a victim at some point. Get over it and choose to be a victor.

You may ask, how do you transition to living life as a victor and not a victim? Remember it starts in your mind. Tell yourself *I don't have to be bound by the bad things that happened to me. That bad situation or circumstance does not define me or dictate the rest of my life. I am more than that incident. I am a victor and not a victim*. Begin to think these words about yourself and say them out loud. Look into the mirror and tell yourself: *I am a victor and not a victim*. Don't get stuck in the past. You can be victorious and live every moment to the fullest, expecting good things to happen!

You may be thinking, "Well those words are not true for me." I understand they may not be true *yet*, but I also understand that words have power (as previously mentioned in the Introduction) and we tend to live our life according to the words spoken to us and over us. Take advantage of this access to the power of words and begin to speak positivity and victory over your life. *I am a victor!*

#69 Laugh at Yourself

Don't be so easily offended and take yourself so seriously. Learn to laugh at yourself like you would at others. It's so freeing. For example, if you're friends laugh at your hair because it turned out funny, you can laugh too! You know it don't look right anyway, so don't get offended if they point it out and make a joke about it. Laugh!

#70 Treat All People with Respect

Be honest. Are you one of those women who goes to a restaurant and has a major attitude with the waitress, just because? Instead of being rude and treating her as if she is nothing, try saying *thank you* and *please* next time. Try smiling at her. Try to be patient if she forgets to bring the hot sauce to the table. Try to not be rude if your order didn't come out right. People make mistakes, including you, so give her a little slack. And finally, leave her a nice tip. How you treat others, you will be treated. Think about this when you get on the campus bus or come into contact with the woman who cleans the dorm bathrooms. Speak to the driver. Say good morning to the janitor. Thank them for their service!

#71 Don't Blame Her

Is she sleeping with your boo? Then maybe he ain't really your boo. More than likely she did not force him to lay down with her. More than likely he laid with her willingly. So, don't be angry with her. Be mad at him.

It seems like most women I know get mad at and seek revenge against the woman our guy cheated on us with instead getting mad at him. He's the one you're in relationship with, not her. He's the one who made you the promises, not her. So, don't blame her. Blame him. Then get a clue and move on. Don't be a fool. Break up with him. He doesn't deserve to be in a relationship with you.

#72 She Is Not Your Competitor

Throughout my life, lots of Black women stare me up

and down and roll their eyes at me. And if I am honest, I'm sure I've done it too. We give that look as if to say, *she think she cute*. Why are we as Black women so competitive? Why do we feel like we have to be "the flyest" woman in the room? When a woman walks in the room who we THINK looks better than us or who has men checking her out, why do we roll our eyes at her or avoid speaking to her? There's enough space in the room for more than one beautiful woman. We can all be "the beautiful woman" in the room and at the same time appreciate the beauty and uniqueness of others. The next time *that* woman walks in the room and you start to look her up and down and roll your eyes, stop yourself and ask *why do I feel threatened by her?* The source of this feeling may be insecurity. If so, choose to recognize that you are insecure and seek help. Read books that will build you up. Possibly invest some time to speak with a counselor. Speak to a trustworthy adult who can offer you advice on overcoming insecurities. And ultimately learn to love yourself—all of yourself, not just parts.

Then take it a step further. Compliment her. Tell her how fly she looks. Engaging with her could be a really powerful antidote for overcoming your insecurities. It's almost magical! It shows you that you're a big girl with big girl panties on! Good job.

#73 Stop Playing Games

I know—you're too scared to show your heart because you are tired of being burned. So instead, you play games. And we all know that when games are played, one person will win, and one person will lose. It's inevitable. And you, being the person that you are, will definitely not be the loser—right? You've been there, done that. You've learned the tricks of the game, and you know how to triumph over the dudes. So, you tuck your heart away—way down deep, instead of being the caring and free-spirited person you were created to be, thinking that that will keep you from getting hurt. You don't trust anyone, your quick to jump to conclusions, you're quick to get angry, you don't forgive or give others the benefit of the doubt, you tell partial truths or just lie straight out, you pretend that things don't bother you when they do, and the list goes on. I'll let you in on a little secret: when it's all said and done, playing games hurts just as bad as a wounded heart, because you never truly get to be yourself. It's always a facade—always a fictional, badass version of you. No one knows who you really are, because *you* are always covering *you* up. Hell, you don't even know who *you* are. You're so busy hiding behind a form of yourself or behind what you want to project that you don't have the opportunity to get to know yourself. Either way, a loss is at stake.

Be you! Stop foolin' around and be true to yourself. If you're silly, be silly. If you like someone, just tell them. You can't be scared that they won't like you back. If you like country music, listen to it. If you don't like the relationship you're in, get out of it; you don't have to stay just because you look good together on social media. If you're part White, own it. End the pretense and the games and just be *you*.

#74 Smile
Smile today. Decide to smile at a minimum of ten people throughout the day—strangers or not. It will brighten their day and yours.

#75 You are More than Your Body and So is He
Stop looking for a man based upon the size of his private package. If this is something you do, raise your standards. Want more out of a relationship than just that.

On the flip side, stop encouraging guys to want you based upon how big your booty is. You are more than your butt.

#76 Feeling Overlooked

Do you ever feel overlooked? That no one notices you or acknowledges you or your contributions? Does it ever seem like there's always certain people who get recognized because of something they have done, but your contributions, time and time again go unnoticed? Well, God notices you. He sees you and he appreciates you. And at the right time, you will be publicly recognized for your impact. Don't make the mistake of forcing people to notice you—you will more than likely end up embarrassing yourself. When you are not receiving recognition, it could be that God is trying to build humility in you.

Should we want the praises or the applauds from people or from God? The only thing people can do is pat you on the back and possibly give you a promotion, but God can promote you and bless you in ways that people cannot. He can put you on a pedestal for everyone to see, but only when he thinks it's best. So, keep doing what is right. Keep helping people. Keep making an impact. Keep giving. Keep doing your best in every area of your life. God sees you, and at the appointed time he will show you off.

#77 He Should Compliment You, Not Complete You

You don't need a man to complete you. He should be a bonus, a compliment—an addition to what you already have going on. He should be the dessert not the meat and veggies. When you place a man at the center of your life, your life will be off-balance. God should be at the center and then everything else will line up. You may ask, how do you make God the center? Do for God what you would do for that man. Give him your life, tell Him your dreams, tell him and show him you love him, spend time alone with him, talk to him, listen to him, wake up thinking about him, and go to bed thanking him. Allow your life to honor him. When God is at the center, he will bring the right man into your life and at the right time and for the right reasons.

#78 Soul Ties

Did you know that when you have sex with someone, it's more than a physical thing? It's spiritual too. In other words, not only do your body parts become intertwined with theirs but so does your spirit with their spirit. Before I continue, I want to make sure you understand that you are more than just your body. Our body is just a shell or a home for our spirit. Our spirit is who we are. Therefore, you must be selective with whom you allow your spirit to be intimate with.

If you choose to lay down with various men or women, it could leave you on the brink of insanity. Why? Because you have meshed your spirit with other peoples' spirits, some of whom you don't even know that well and are not sure where they are at spiritually and mentally. By the time you have sex with several people, you don't even know who you are anymore; you are all mixed up because your spirit has been tainted with so many others'. Most people I know didn't become crazy until their sex life launched and soared. What do I mean by crazy? Someone who seems to be emotionally or mentally unstable and who seems to always have some sort of drama going on.

Maybe you've only had sex with one or two people, but what if those couple of people you had sex with had sex with 30 other people? Those one or two people can intoxicate you with all those befuddled spirits. And how many people did those 30 individuals have sex with? So even though you may have only ever had one or two sex partners, in the spirit realm you may have had sex with like 400 people. That's why you don't know who you are. You're confused and perplexed. Sometimes you feel like you're about to lose it. That may be why you call yourself *b**ch*, because you don't have sense enough to know that you are a woman, fearlessly and wonderfully created by God.

If this is the path you are on, you have the power to stop it if you so desire and choose stability and sanity. I did. You can too.

#79 Temporary Thrill

Stop letting these guys convince you to be involved in a three-some, 4-some or more-some. It may feel good, exciting, sexy, hot, desirable, and unbelievably incredible for the time, but trust me, nothing beneficial can come from that. Shame, guilt, and drama are the more likely outcomes. Nothing good can come of that. Nothing! Stop being so easy. So naïve. So stupid. Remember #61 from this syllabus—have some lines in your life, some things you just won't do!

#80 Leave

A man cannot love you *and* abuse you. The two cannot co-exist. That's physical, mental, and verbal abuse, or any other abuse. Love and abuse are like oil and water—they don't mix together. So leave. Please leave.

#81 Sex is Not an Antidote to Loneliness

Sometimes we as women lay with men not because we want to, but because we are lonely. We feel that having sex will fill our void and help us to feel warm and loved and befriended. But if you are not in a committed relationship, the experience with him can make you feel even lonelier because sex was not designed to bring love or to eliminate loneliness. Sex was designed to enhance an already loving and committed marriage. It was meant to bring the two individuals closer together to a level of intimacy no one else can fulfill. When sex is used to fill the void of loneliness or depression it only multiplies those feelings.

#82 Thirsty

Have you chosen to be with someone who is not doing anything with their life? Have you decided to be with a man who is married? Have you decided to be with a man that you know, deep down inside, is on the down low? Sometimes, we as women know a person is not right for us, but we choose to ignore it because we'd rather be with someone than be alone. Sometimes we desire to be booed up so badly or we just hate the idea of being alone that we get with anyone. Or sometimes, we get to the point where we don't want to face our family, aunts and uncles and other relatives, only for them to keep questioning us with, "You don't have a boyfriend YET?" Don't lower your standards to satisfy other people's desires for you. Those people can't live your life for you. They have a hard-enough time living their own lives, let alone yours too. Don't lower your standards because you are lonely. Loneliness can cause us to do stupid things. Take the time to write out a list of healthy hobbies you enjoy. That way, when you get lonely you can pull out the list and choose one to occupy your time with. Write down a list of family and friends who love you that you can call or spend time with instead of feeling alone. Don't allow loneliness to lead you into detrimental situations. It's not worth it.

Did you ever consider other people who may be lonely? Do you know any widows that you can invite to lunch? Do you know of any elderly people at your church who you can stop by and visit or give a call to? Do you know someone who always walks alone on campus that you can reach out to and study with? Sometimes when you get your mind off of yourself and think of how you can be there for someone else, it lifts your spirit.

#83 Dat's My Nigga

Do you date "niggas" or do you date men? Be honest. All a "nigga" can do is tear you down. They may be fine and sexy, and they may have all the swag in the world, but all in all, the term is derived from the word *nigger*, which means stupid. But far more than that, the term carries blame, shame, disgrace, abuse, dehumanization, humiliation, insufficiency, contempt and rejection, which throughout American history has been dumped onto the Black race. Therefore, the modern term "nigga" is usually referring to a Black man who has decided to live with that burden, because it is easier for him to stay there than to take the necessary steps to be free from degradation. Do you want to fall into that debased pit with him? Stop thinking you can change him. You won't. Leave him. Pray for him. Choose better.

#84 The Vicious Cycle

Ever wonder why you keep dating the same man? I mean, not actually the **same** man, but the same **type** of man. The last one's name was Chris, this one's name is Dion, and the next one's name will be Tre. But they may as well all have the same name because they all act the same and treat you pretty much the same way. They all seem to be "niggas". (See #83) You want to know why you keep dating the same type of guy over and over again and never attracting someone different? You wanna know why you keep dating niggas? It has nothing to do with them.

What do all these men have in common? That's right, YOU. They all dated **you**. **You** are the common denominator in all the relationships. Evidently, this tends to be the type of guy you attract. There is something in you that needs to change so that this type of man is no longer drawn to you. Most guys know when a woman is insecure and know what they can get away with. If you are strong, confident, and exude a loving spirit, more than likely that type of guy won't even look your way because he knows he cannot get away with treating you like crap.

In order to get rid of this indicator that attracts the wrong type of guy to you, you must give your life to God and ask him to change you from the inside out. Ask him to create in you a clean heart and allow him to love on you and love all the dark areas of your life away and make them bright again. Allow God to help you be the beautiful woman that he created you to be. Then ask him to bring the right guy into your life. Seek God first, allow him to love on you and make you whole. Then you will be more prepared to be a wonderful partner when God blesses you with a good man.

I know firsthand for this to be true. I dated Chris, Dion, and Tre. It was like going from one hell to the next. Finally, I gave my life to Christ. He began to change me and mold me into the woman he had in mind. I no longer attracted "niggas". I began to attract men who would love me and treat me right, because I had started loving myself. And the only way you can properly love yourself is to love your Creator and to live for him. Now, I am married to Leonard, my king.

I can honestly say because I am with Leonard, I am a better me. Ask yourself, *does the guy you are with bring out the best in you, or the worse?* Choose better.

#85 Playing House
Are you "shacking up?" (*Shacking up*-an old school term for living with your partner.) Or are you considering doing so? I strongly encourage you not to. I believe the definition of the word *shack* is enough indication as to why it's not a good idea.

shack: *noun.* An unstable dwelling place, a small house most commonly in a state of disrepair.

Choose better.

Many people choose to "shack up" or "play house" because they either don't want to get married but want all the benefits of marriage OR they want to practice and see if it's going to work out before getting married OR they want to save money on rent. All three reasons sound like legitimate reasons. However, the main reason I don't recommend it (besides it not being God-ordained) is that it points directly to the definition of a "shack"—*it's unstable*. I may be wrong, but I feel that it is impossible for either person to ever feel completely stable. To me, this set up always poses the questions: *Will this last?* and *Is my partner fully committed?*

Also, if you think that moving in with someone will make them commit to marriage faster, it usually doesn't. Why would someone go through all the trouble of marriage and the level of commitment that a marriage requires, if they can have the trappings of marriage without the commitment? Don't fool yourself. Don't take what may seem like the easy way out to get to what you really want. If marriage is what you want, then wait for marriage. Don't settle for less.

Also, if you find out that you don't want to be with your partner for the rest of your life, it's harder to break up and move on if you live with them, than if you don't. Don't worry, if you date someone long enough, you'll be able to tell if they are good for you or not. If you can't tell if a person is good for you or not, ask yourself these questions: *Do they bring out the best in me? Am I a better person because of them? Do I bring out the best in them? Are they better because of me?* If you answered *yes* to any of those questions, then you may be with a suitable person. But if you answered *no* to those questions, you may want to consider separating yourself from your partner. And remember, that's easier to do if you don't live with them.

#86 He is Not Your Father

Are you trying to fill the void that your father may have created with attention and affection from another man? If your father hurt you in anyway, I strongly encourage you to seek counseling and receive healing from those hurts as soon as possible, especially before engaging in a serious relationship. No man can fill that void. Instead, you become a weight around his neck, because you will constantly require things of him that he cannot provide and that is not fair to him. He is not your father. And a man is not meant to complete you, but to love you.

#87 The Wedding Gift

This section is not meant to make you feel shame but instead to reveal to you the truth about the damaging effects of premarital sex. And just to be clear, this applies to the men as well...

Have you ever received a gift in a beautiful box, wrapped in stunning paper, adorned with an eloquent bow? It's something that just about everyone would love to receive, and be told, "just for you."

Well I want you, for a moment, to think of yourself as that specially wrapped gift. Now when you get married, wouldn't it be wonderful to be able to present this gift, *yourself*, to your husband and say, "Just for you?" Do you think he would appreciate and value such a gift? Or do you think he would rather receive a gift that has been opened before, or the packaging has been ripped off and then re-taped in the attempt to make it look unused? Is that the gift you would want to present to your future spouse? You and your body represent that gift—a gift that God created just for you to share with your future husband. God intended for his body to be a gift to you, the wife, as well. Neither body, his nor yours, was meant to be opened and used and wrapped back up again before presenting to each other.

God tells us to abstain from sex until marriage so that it can be something special that only the two of you have shared together. Just like wedding guests bring gifts to the reception for the bride and groom to open after the festivities, I believe God brings gifts to the reception as well. One of those gifts is sex. Hot, heavy, intimate, passionate, spirit-filled sex—with no limitations!

You don't want to have to compare your husband with others who have come before him, and you don't want him to have to do the same.

If you really want to get married one day, and you desire a healthy satisfying relationship, then think about how precious your gift is before you let somebody else use it again. And yes, this applies to men as well.

If your special gift has already been opened and used, it's never too late for restoration. Again, what I wrote above was not meant to make you feel shame but instead to reveal to you the truth about the damaging effects of premarital sex. The truth will set you free. All you must do is recognize the truth—recognize where you may have done wrong and then choose to do things differently. Choosing a different path doesn't bring about better results right away. It's a process. But the process to restoration and healing is worth it.

How do you begin this process? Try the following steps:

1. Recognize that you have used your gift in the wrong way
2. Ask God to forgive you and to restore you
3. Make a commitment to be celibate
4. Get some accountability partners to help you
5. Read books that will encourage you on this journey
6. Refrain from watching movies and listening to music that feed your sexual desires
7. If you make a mistake and have sex, forgive yourself and continue the journey. It's okay. God's got you. He loves you whether you make a mistake or not. His love never changes. He only wants the best for you!

Remember God is able to do anything, including restoration. Just ask.

restoration: *noun.* The act of returning something to a former owner, place or condition.

#88 Think About It

This is a continuation of *#87 The Wedding Gift*. Think about it... if everyone did as God commanded and married one person and stayed committed to that one person for the remainder of their life, there would not be any sexually transmitted diseases and no children without parents. But of course, we are human, and we do things our own way. We can't continue to do things our way and expect God's results.

#89 Baggage Claim

When your gift has been used over and over again by men (or by women) and you get married, and your future husband's gift to you has been used over and over again by women (or by men) before marrying you—you enter the marriage with what people like to call "baggage". Your marriage *can* work, however the baggage is heavy and often gets in the way. Avoid lugging baggage into your future by not being intimate with everyone you date or tweet. However, if you do happen to take this kind of baggage into your marriage, and so does your spouse, be willing to **unpack** the bags. In other words, talk about the hard stuff with your spouse, which includes the shame, guilt, or other tough areas that may stem from your background. Work through it no matter how painful it may be. Get marital counseling if and when necessary. Read books that can help with this. All in all, don't ignore the baggage. Don't ignore the damage that comes from premarital sex. Instead, choose to acknowledge it. Claim it and proceed to unpack it. Let it go.

#90 Safe Sex?

Condoms can protect you from getting pregnant and from contracting a sexually transmitted disease, but they cannot protect you from a broken heart. Choose to protect your heart and your spirit. You do not have to have sex with everyone you meet, or with everyone that turns you on, or with everyone who takes you out for a good time. You don't owe your date sex. Condoms provide an illusion of safe sex because they protect your physical body, but they do not protect your mind, your emotions, and your spirit which often get damaged when being involved sexually with someone.

#91 STD's Around Campus

Herpes. Gonorrhea. Hepatitis. Chlamydia. Bacterial Vaginosis. Syphilis. Trichomoniasis. HIV. These diseases and more are on your campus. Do you or did you have one of these sexually transmitted diseases? If so, I am truly sorry that you had to deal with such a nasty disease. If you contracted one of these or another STD because you were sexually assaulted, that is even more painful, and again, I am sorry that that happened to you. If you contracted one of these from your partner because they were creeping, I am sincerely sorry as well. If you contracted one of these from "just some guy" or "just some girl" then I am again, sorry that this has happened to you. Whenever possible, remember to make wise choices about sex. Consider what's at stake every time. Remember you can contract a STD via oral sex as well.

I believe God designed sex for a healthy, loving marriage. It should not occur before marriage. Whether you live by the Bible or not, abstinence just makes good sense. Just think, if everybody, I mean EVERYBODY dated and waited patiently until they found the right person to marry, saved sex for marriage, and then after marrying stayed with that one person "till death do them part,"—there would more than likely be no such thing as sexually transmitted diseases. No issues. Just good ole sex.

Unfortunately, we humans often don't exercise self-control. We *have* self-control, but we opt not to use it. Instead, we do what we want to do. We do what makes us feel good. But then we get upset or even depressed when the consequences of our choices affect us negatively. Remember a series of poor choices will lead to an overall menial life and a series of good choices will lead to an overall satisfying and even exceptional life.

#92 An STD Doesn't Make You Trash

If you have a sexually transmitted disease (STD) you are not worthless. You are not trash. You are not damaged goods. Don't go throw your life away because you think *no one will ever want to be with me now* or *no one will ever love me now* or *no one will ever want to touch me now.* That's simply not the truth. The truth is you **have** a disease. You **are not** a disease. You may have it, but it shouldn't have you. Find out what you can do to treat the symptoms or eliminate them if possible. Eat healthy foods. Drink lots of water. Exercise. Get sufficient rest. All of these things matter. Take a day at a time and decide to make the necessary choices so that you don't spread it to anyone else and so that you don't contract another one.

#93 An STD Shouldn't Make You Careless

Don't be one of those females who contracts a STD and decides—*who cares about life, I'm just going to have fun and have sex with whomever I so desire, and who cares if I pass the STD around. The person who gave it to me didn't care, so why should I care about someone else?* That's just plain evil. If you know you have a disease and you know you are capable of passing it on, don't have sex until you get treated. Don't be foul and pass it on just because you don't care. The truth is, you DO care. More than likely you're just angry and hurt and that's usually what hurt and angry people do. Hurt and angry people seek revenge, even at the cost of innocent people. Don't stoop. Let the other person know that you have it, because that's only fair. Get the necessary help that you need to live a healthy and happy life—it's still possible.

#94 Limit: One Baby Daddy

Do you have a baby daddy? ...Don't make the same mistake twice. Don't go and get yourself *another* baby daddy. You don't need more trouble. Do something different this time. Choose **not** to sleep with the next guy. If you do, use a condom—prevent another baby daddy situation.

#95 T.H.O.T

Be honest. Have you ever felt disappointed or upset when you walked into a room full of people and you discovered that you were not the finest woman in the room? Or that there was another woman there who was prettier than you and everyone was looking at her? Or another woman whose hair was flawless, and people were constantly complimenting her? Or another who had a better shape than you and the men were checking her out? Did your skin just crawl? Were you mad that she was there? Was she hogging the attention that you were expecting to get? If you are honest and you answered yes to any of the questions above, then you are not alone. It's just that most women will never admit it. You need to know that no matter who else is in the room, YOU are beautiful, and YOU are special. God made YOU just the way he wanted you to be and he wasn't having a bad day when he made you. Your nose, your hair, your skin, your shape, your smile, everything about you is what makes you unique. God knew what he was doing when he made you. Don't worry about who else is in the room. Be happy with yourself. Be confident and be kind and you will automatically shine.

#96 Stop Comparing

One of my favorite quotes of all time is, *Comparison is a thief of joy.* (-Theodore Roosevelt)

Stop comparing yourself to others. It only hurts you. It rapes you of your joy. You can only be you, and that is enough.

I understand that it's difficult not to compare yourself to others. If you're like me, you may have tried to stop but you tend to fail often. One of the ways I've learned to combat the tendency to compare myself with others is to speak affirmations about myself. Before I step out of the house each morning or on my way to work, I affirm myself out loud. I say what I know about myself to be true and include the things I am working to improve upon as well. Here's what I tell myself out loud every morning:

I am beautiful.
I am blessed.
I am enough.
I am loved.
I am loving.
I am generous.
I am intelligent.

I am successful.

I am ready.

I am bold.

I am wise.

I am not easily angered.

I am forgiven.

I am forgiving.

I am fun to be around.

I am confident.

I am a child of the most-high God.

Listing these affirmations (and more) out loud reassures me that I am special and that although other people are also special, that doesn't take away from who I am. There is enough room for everyone to be special and for everyone to shine!

#97 Stop Being Selfish

Don't allow the tune that goes "me-me-me-me-meeee" to be your theme song. You have to know and realize sooner than later that *it's not all about ME.* If you live with the mindset that it's all about you, you will be a most unhappy camper. Life will not always move to the beat of your personal drum. Life will not stick to your agenda. And you have to learn to be okay with that.

Choose to wake up in the morning and not let yourself be the first thing on your mind. Instead, thank God for waking you up and ask him if there is anything you can do *for him* today. Ask him to put someone in your path that you can help or be a blessing to that day. If you get your focus off yourself and off your own agenda and off your own problems, you will begin to enjoy life more.

We need others to bring fulfillment to our lives and they need us. If we all got up and sang the melody to "me-me-me-me-meeee" the world would be off balance and we would be frustrated with life. We were made to co-exist and that includes thinking of others and being a blessing to them. That could include something as small as connecting with someone and saying, "Hello, I was thinking about you". Or it could mean giving someone a ride when they need it, or blessing someone with a financial gift. Remember though, that helping someone else often requires sacrifice and inconveniencing yourself. It won't always fit perfectly into your schedule. But when you help someone else or gift them with something, it just feels good. When you open yourself up to be a blessing to others, get ready, because you will be blessed in return!

#98 Dream Team

Surround yourself with people who are moving forward—with hard-working, successful people and you will inevitably move forward. Surround yourself with people who are moving backward, and inescapably so will you.

Surround yourself with people who are positively impacting your life. Remove yourself from those who don't.

Avoid Losers. Hang with Dreamers and Doers.

Who are your friends?

MIDTERM

Grab your journal and respond to the following questions.

1. Write about something that came up for you.
2. What's something you realize that you like about yourself?
3. What's something you'd like to change about yourself?
4. What's something you like about the relationships you're in?
5. What's something you want to change about the relationships you're in?

PART 3
ACADEMIC DEVELOPMENT

#99 Keys to Academic Success, Part I

Be sure to do all of the following to ensure academic success:

- Go to class
- Buy the books
- Listen in class
- Take good notes
- Read the assigned reading
- Put your phone away in class
- Put your phone away when you study
- Study—alone *and* in study groups
- Reread your notes
- Meet the professor
- Shake his or her hand
- Keep your head up and make eye contact when you talk to him or her
- Raise your hand in class
- Ask questions—including the dumb ones
- Go to professors' office hours

- Go to tutoring
- Go to your discussion class
- *Reread your notes*
- Stay awake
- Do your absolute best
- Ask for help
- Find out what resources are available to you as a student
- Use them
- Persevere
- Finish

#100 Keys to Academic Success, Part II

As a first-generation student at UCLA, there were many aspects of college that I had no clue about. I did not know how to navigate the system. Of all the items listed in *Academic Success, Part I*, I only knew to do a few of them. No one told me those things, and if and when they did, either I didn't listen, or I didn't understand the significance of it all. Such as going to professor's office hours—it's a must. Even if you don't see the need—go. Introduce yourself. Ask them questions about their career and what led them to where they are today. Ask them for any tips for how to finish school and be prepared for the real world. Most professors appreciate when students value their opinion. When it comes time for grading, they will more than likely remember you. If your grade is on the line between a B+ and an A-, you'll more than likely get the A- just because they remember you and your effort to do well.

#101 Get an Internship While in College

Get you an internship! An absolute must during your college career, is to apply and interview for internships, even if they are not paid positions—get the experience! If you need the money, work an extra job on the side. Do the internship over the summer instead of summer school or in addition to, if absolutely necessary. After you graduate and are in search of that first real job, a 3.0 GPA with experience in that field will get you further than a 3.7 GPA with no experience at all. Go after internships. Apply. Apply. Apply.

#102 Study Abroad! Be a Global Learner!

Next, do a semester abroad, or a summer abroad. Study in South Africa. Study in Italy. Study in Japan. Study in Guatemala. Study in Mexico. Study across the country. Get the exposure. It opens your eyes to the world around you and not just the campus around you. Exposure does volumes for a person's life, expectations, dreams, and career. When you start your job recruitment, you are more likely to be hired with a 2.9 GPA and a semester abroad in China than the student who stayed on campus all four years, spent her summers taking classes, and got a 4.0 GPA! Explore the world—it's a wondrous thing. You can't afford it, you say? Apply for a grant. Search for scholarships. Take out a loan. You take out loans to buy cars, clothes, and hair. So why not do so to invest in your future?

Gaining global experience will help you be able to do the following which could open the door for more gainful employment opportunities:

1. solve problems
2. be emotionally intelligent
3. manage a project
4. thrive in ambiguity
5. understand cultural differences
6. apply global experience to any situation

Also, studying and traveling globally will help you to expand your job recruitment list by realizing that career opportunities are global and not just in your city, your state or even this country.

Think big. Go global!

#103 How to Handle Racist Professors

Cuss them out! No. I'm just playing. Cuss them out in your head, but fareal—report them. If it's something overt and impacts your studies, report them. Write an email to the campus climate office at your school and let them know exactly what happened, including who was involved, and any necessary details such as, dates and locations. Also, send an email to the professor letting them know how they were racist. Copy your advisor, counselor, or parent to the email so that others have record of how you respectfully informed the professor of his or her racist actions or words. However, if they make an "everyday racist offense," aka a microaggression (where they make an ignorant comment that didn't really alter your experience, but it simply let you know who they are) just shake your head and keep it moving. Get your A (or your B) and keep it moving. You will have racist professors. Even Black professors can exhibit racism, also known as self-hatred. But if it doesn't really impact your interaction with the professor or your grade, just let it go. Some battles are not worth it.

#104 Is Graduate School for Me?

Figure out if graduate school is for you. Talk to people in the field you want to pursue and find out what they did. When they graduated it may not have been necessary at that time to have a master's degree, but times have changed, and you may need to continue on to secondary education. Do the research early on and find out. Start engaging professors and other university staff so when it is time to apply to graduate school, they will be able to write you a remarkable letter of recommendation which will help secure you a spot at one of your desired schools. Apply to more than just one grad school. Don't drop all your eggs in one basket. Have options. Be willing to move across the country to obtain your master's degree. Don't be afraid of the cold or a different culture or of being further away from your family. Your family is just a plane ride away. Go be a big girl and do big things. You can handle it!

#105 College is a Journey

See what else is available to you while you are a student. Meet people you wouldn't ordinarily meet. Ask questions. Meet people you admire. Ask how they got to where they are today. Figure out what you need to do and do it. And enjoy the journey! Remember journeys have twists and turns and dips and bumps and hills and valleys. The road is not usually a smooth road. Those obstacles are there only to bring out the best in you, to help you grow up, and to prepare you for what is next in life. Keep going, keep pressing. Pause and rest at the rest stops along the way and be sure to fuel up, just keep going. You can do it!

PART 4
MISCELLANEOUS ITEMS

#106 The Power of Your Words: The Spiritual Realm

Words have power. Did you know that the words that come out of your mouth can influence your life? This may sound ridiculous, but consider this concept... In the spirit realm, it looks like this: pretend for a moment that you are in your dorm room. And in that room, lined up along all four walls (next to your bookcases and bed and desk) are spiritual beings, bad ones and good ones. You can't see them, but just imagine they are there. Now say you're sitting at your desk, your laptop is open, but your eyes are starting to slowly glaze over. If you say something like, *I can't finish this work, it's too hard*, then all the negative spirits peel off the wall, and without you being able to see them working, they do everything in their power to keep you from finishing your work. All the sudden the bed looks so appealing, or the blinking light on your phone grabs your attention, or Netflix screams your name, and you can't resist. Don't give the bad guys power to prevent you from completing your work. It may sound silly, but realistically speaking if you say the words, *I can't* or *it's too hard*, then your study hour is probably ending. Before you said, *I can't*—the evil spirits had no power; they could not keep you from taking care of your responsibilities. But as soon as you said it, you gave them permission to come in and take over your time. The point is, once you say, *I can't* to something that you need to do and that you can do, but maybe don't have the desire to do at the time, you give evil forces power to cause all sorts of distractions and discouragement can creep in so that you CAN'T get it done.

However, if you say, "This homework may be challenging, but I can do it"—you give the good guys (or girls 😊) power to encourage you in one or more possible ways:

- Adopt better study habits
- Call a friend and ask for help
- "*Wo*-man up" and simply get it done
- Activate self-control and choose not to go out that night, but stay at home and study
- Choose to pray and ask God for knowledge, wisdom, and strength to help you accomplish what you need to do

What you speak from your mouth has power over your life.

#107 The Power of Your Words: I AM
Instead of saying degrading things about yourself, stop yourself mid-sentence and say positive things about yourself aloud. Here are some suggestions of positive affirmations you can say out loud:

- *I am loved*
- *I am beautiful*
- *I am successful*
- *I am worthy*
- *I am blessed*
- *I am responsible*
- *I am kind*
- *I am fun to be around*
- *I am healed*
- *I am healthy*
- *I am whole*
- *I am forgiven*
- *I am intelligent*

Even if you don't believe these things about yourself at the time, remember, WORDS HAVE POWER! And just as negative consequences can come as a result of negative words, so can positive results come as a result of thinking and saying positive things. Use the list of affirmations above for your benefit.

#108 Music is a Spirit

What music are you listening to? When I was in college, one of my favorite songs was *B**ches Ain't Sh*t*. Thugged-out rap artists from the 80's and 90's are who I constantly listened to in my ride and on the stereo. I loved their songs. I knew most of the lyrics and club nights were the bomb (or shall I say lit) when these songs played one after the other. At that point in my life, however, I didn't know that WORDS HAVE POWER. The lyrics I was listening to over and over were being embedded in my mind, and in my heart, and ultimately in my life. In many ways my life mirrored those verses and choruses without me even realizing it. The lyrics were feeding me and before I knew it, I was often the *b**ch* in their song. Never was that my intent when absorbing that music, but again, I didn't know that the words were planting degrading seeds within me. Listening to those songs repetitively were normalizing things that I never would have imagined myself to be associated with. I found myself in situations and circumstances that resembled the hard-core songs, that I knew better than to be involved in—but I was.

What are you listening to?

What does your life look like?
Are there any parallels?

Do you realize that White people in America and Europe control the Black music industry? You may see Black faces and hear Black voices, but it's usually controlled by White people. Racist White people. They support and fund the raunchy and degrading lyrics over the positive and uplifting ones. It's easier for artists to get a record deal and more profitable for those who rap and sing about murder, drugs, ménage á trois, b**ches and hoes than it is for those who rap about peace, justice and love. Throughout American history, White people have often found creative ways to dehumanize Black people. Music is just another method. Don't fall for it!

#109 Money Ain't Everything

Money ain't everything. It's definitely essential for living, but let it have its proper place in your life. It should not control your choices. It should not be your ultimate goal in life. Let your dreams and passions lead you to your purpose, not the desire to be rich. Money can come and go, but your passion (coupled with good choices) will lead you to true success.

#110 The Biblical Meaning of Love

What is love? That word gets thrown around a lot, but do we really know what we are declaring when we say we love someone? My Bible tells me that *love is patient, love is kind, love is not easily angered, it is not puffed up, it does not keep record of wrongs, it is not jealous. It does not dishonor others; it is not self-seeking. Love does not delight in evil but in the truth. Love always protects, always trusts, always hopes, always perseveres.*

This meaning of love is so powerful and so complete. I used to tell my husband I loved him, but it was often based on how he made me feel. If he was giving me what I needed and if I got my way, then it was easy for me to love him. Love should not be contingent upon how someone makes you feel. Love is bigger than your feelings.

When I recall how I treated my husband when things weren't going my way, I realize now that I wasn't loving him at all, according to scripture. I always got angry and I always recalled what he did to hurt my feelings. But in this passage of scripture it says love does not keep record of wrongs, nor is it easily angered. Wow. I realized I had a lot to learn about love. I decided to stop telling my husband that I loved him so much and instead asked God to help me to show love. I wanted to be kind and patient. I wanted to protect him and not harm him. I wanted our love for each other to persevere.

And then I wanted to be able to love others more authentically. Love is a powerful entity that can restore, heal, and make better. I didn't want to misuse or abuse the word anymore. I wanted to love the way it instructed in scripture. I am still on that journey of learning to love more completely. I encourage you to look at the people in your life that you love. Then ask yourself *am I loving them according to God's word*? If not, then ask God to help you to love the way He loves. It's not easy, but it's possible and it's extremely rewarding. Join me on this journey of love! Choose better.

CONCLUSION

If I have offended you in any way, it's possible that you have been convicted. Or maybe I just offended you—not my intent. Either way, hopefully, you realize there are some areas in your life that can use some work. Don't worry, we all need work, myself included. You're not alone. But don't run from the work. Choose to work. It's so worth it. I'm not asking you to agree with everything I've written. Just consider it. It was all for the sake of love. I am still learning and figuring things out as well.

God loves you so much. He has so much more for you. If you don't believe me, then just say these words and mean it: "God, if you love me, show me." If you said those words and meant them, get ready for his love to wrap around you and change your life. Remember, choose better.

Being yourself is not just okay; it's necessary.
                                        -Ashly Okoli

(Ashli is one of the UT students I was blessed to work with through FLI.)

FINAL EXAM

Grab your journal and respond to the following questions.

1. What are you going to do differently?
2. Who can you seek for assistance?
3. Do you believe God loves you? Why or why not?
4. Write down your short-term goals.
5. Write down your long-term goals.
6. What is the first step in pursuing your goals?

PART 5
A LITTLE SOMETHING EXTRA

AUTHOR'S STORY

When God saved me from myself, from self-destruction, I was 21 years old. I was depressed and did not want to live anymore. I thought of ways to end my life, but I was too scared to do so because I had always been taught that if you commit suicide you will go straight to hell. So, I just lived in a state of torment, living, but wanting to die. I had grown up in church but based upon how my life had turned out at that point I wasn't sure if God was real and I thought if he was, he definitely didn't love *me*. I was wrong. I now realize that many of life's hardships were because of the poor choices that I made. I made excuses for my poor choices saying that if my father hadn't done what he did, then I wouldn't be like this. I hadn't learned yet how to take responsibility for my life and not allow *what happened to me* to be the determining factor in my choices.

I was 21 and I hated life. I had been through emotional, physical, and sexual abuse at the hands of others, which led to my own alcohol abuse. I was mean and angry and full of bitterness and rage. One day I had the courage to share with someone what I was experiencing. I told the details of my life to an older lady at church. She encouraged me to go home that night and lay prostrate (to lay on the ground, facing the ground, in complete submission and reverence) and cry out to God and tell him everything I had told her.

I went home and did as she said. I felt stupid, but I figured at that point I had nothing to lose. I told God all the horrible things that had happened to me since I was 5 years old and how I felt like he didn't love me, and that I no longer wanted to live. I talked to him for a long time that night and then I cried myself to sleep right there on the floor.

The next morning, my roommate and I went body surfing at Venice Beach like we did almost every day that summer. We were both students at UCLA and enjoyed being so close to the beach. We would swim way out to where the water was extremely deep so that we could catch the big waves and ride them to shore.

This particular day, the waves were huge, but none of them would pick us up and take us to shore. In fact, it seemed that we were gradually getting further and further away from the shore. At first it wasn't a big deal, but when wave after wave passed us by, something felt odd. We looked at some guys who were about 30 feet to the right of us and they looked at us. We all had that look like *something isn't right* written across our faces. Suddenly sirens went off all along the shore and lifeguards grabbed their buoys, ran into the water and started pulling people out. It seemed like the waves started coming faster and harder. We tried catching them but to no avail. Finally, a wave came and took my friend about half-way to shore, but I just kept being pulled further and further out to sea. The lifeguards came and pulled her out of the water, then they went and got the two guys out also.

I saw my friend point towards me, motioning for the lifeguards to come get me. They attempted, but turned around when they realized how far out I was. I tried everything. I tried swimming in; I tried to touch my feet to the bottom, but there was no ocean floor anywhere near; I screamed for help; I struggled and fought with the water, but nothing worked. I didn't realize it at the time, but I was drowning. I was getting tired and no one was coming out to help me. I was as far out in the ocean as where the lifeguard boats usually drive by, but there were no boats that day.

I could feel my spirit leaving my body. I felt like I had started hovering over my body and I could feel myself leaving. Dying. Drowning. Everything around me became eerily quiet. I stopped trying to fight the water. I had almost given up but tried one last thing. I decided to cry out to God—the same God that I felt didn't love me. But I had nothing else to lose but to try. I cried, *God, is this it? Is this the end? I'm only 21 years old. Is this how I am supposed to go? If you love me, please save me.*

At that very moment, not a second later, I saw a man walking towards me. I didn't understand how he was walking—there was no ocean floor within reach. He walked right up to me and reached out his hand to me. I reached back, but a huge wave came and pulled me away from his reach. I cried again, *God if you love me, please save me.* The man came closer and reached for me again. I reached back and he grabbed my hand and pulled me to him. I remember I wrapped my arms around his neck so tightly he had to ask me to let go a little because I was choking him.

He walked me all the way into shore and sat me next to my friend. Immediately the lifeguards ran over to me and were checking my breathing. The man who rescued me stood there for a moment and then began to walk away. "What's your name?" I called to him. "Chris," he responded. "Thank you, Chris." He walked away.

My friend who didn't even believe in God said, "That was an angel." I didn't believe her, even though I was the one who grew up in church.

I heard on the news that afternoon that 13 people drowned along the Pacific Coast that day due to Riptides.

That night I went with my mother to a mass choir rehearsal where people from churches within our denomination from all over L.A. would be there. I had several cousins who were there who I hadn't seen in a while. My mother told me, just as we were getting started to stand up and tell my testimony—*tell the story about how the man rescued you from the tormenting sea*. I told the story about the waves and the man. One of my cousins, who I hadn't seen or spoken to in possibly a year listened intently and then quieted me. "Thaïs, last night, Michelle (her daughter who was not present) dreamed that you drowned in the ocean. Michelle said that God woke her in the middle of the night and told her *pray that I will send an angel to save her*. Thaïs, that man was an angel."

I had no words. I just covered my face and wept. In that moment God answered so many questions I had had the night before when I laid prostrate on the floor. It was as if he was saying to me: *Yes, I love you. And it is not your time to go. You didn't want to live, but it is not your time to go. I have a plan for your life Thaïs. A purpose. I made you for a reason.* That night, I gave my life to God and I have been on a journey with him ever since. I never want to go back to that old life away from him. That life started off fun and exciting but ended in torment and depression. I never want that taste in my mouth again. God loves me and I thank God he allowed his son Jesus to die on the cross to save me from myself! I chose better.

ABOUT THE AUTHOR

Thaïs was born in Los Angeles and grew up in Pasadena, CA. She earned her undergraduate degree from UCLA and her master's from the University of Texas at Austin. She is the youngest of seven children born to Dorris and Barbara Bass. What Thaïs cherishes most is her family including her cousins, aunts & uncles. Her favorite childhood memories include going camping, fishing, and boating with her parents, siblings, and extended family. After graduating from UCLA where she studied African American Studies & English, she started teaching 2nd grade in Compton, CA while studying acting by night at the Beverly Hills Playhouse. Shortly thereafter, she married Leonard Moore and moved to Baton Rouge, LA. There she studied playwriting at LSU and with the help of her husband opened The Black Theatre Company of Baton Rouge where she produced, directed, and acted in many of her own works. During this time, she was also a stay-at-home mother of her three joys, Jaaucklyn, Lauryn, and Leonard. Upon moving to Austin, she studied acting at UT and eventually started working at UT as a program coordinator for a high school outreach program, meanwhile serving as a mentor to many of the students at UT. That one-on-one mentoring sparked an interest in Thaïs to create a holistic development program for Black undergraduate women at UT. Along with her colleague, Dr. Tiffany T. Lewis, she started the internationally known program called the Fearless Leadership Institute. One of her favorite pass times is playing basketball in the front yard with her husband and children.